My Personal Walk
With God 2

My Personal Walk With God 2

Angie Deleston

To order additional copies of this book, contact:
Xlibris Corporation
1-888-795-4274
www.Xlibris.com
Orders@Xlibris.com
37532

Though shalt love the Lord thy God with all thine heart, and with all thy soul, and with all thy might.
                                                                    —Deut. 6:5

Man looketh on the outward appearance, but the Lord looketh on the heart.
                                                                    —I Sam. 16:7

What doth the Lord require of thee, but to do justly, and to love mercy, and to walk humbly with thy God?
                                                                    —Mic. 6:8

Blessed are they which are persecuted for righteousness' sake: for theirs is the kingdom of heaven. Blessed are ye, when men shall revile you, and persecute you, and shall say all manner of evil against you falsely, for my sake. Rejoice, and be exceeding glad: for great is your reward in heaven: for so persecuted they the prophets which were before you.
                                                                    —Matt. 5:3-12

All things work together for good to them that love God.
                                                                    —Rom. 8:28

This is love, that we walk after his commandments.
                                                                    —II John 1:6

Beloved, follow not that which is evil, but that which is good.
                                                                    —III John 1:11

DEDICATION TO MY LORD

I dedicate this book to the Holy Trinity: God the father, Jesus the son, and the Holy Spirit. God, I want to live holy for you because holiness is who you are. Holiness is what I want to be. Transform my mind in your will, and mold my heart in your will because holiness is what I want to be about. "In thee, O Lord, do I put my trust; let me never be ashamed: deliver me in thy righteousness. Bow down thine ear to me; deliver me speedily: be thou my strong rock, for a house of defense to save me" (Ps. 31:1-2). God, I thank you for directing my life. I thank you for blessing me with the family and friends that I have.

God, thank you for the times when I felt alone, you were always there for me. God, I want to thank you for teaching me how to forgive, how to love, how to stand, how to be patient, how to be humble, and most of all, I thank you for teaching me and showing me how to fall in love with you. If you did not spend the time that you spent with me one on one, to let me know it was you, I would have never gotten the chance to know you, and I wouldn't be able to do your work faithfully and know that the things you did for me came directly from your heart. Thank you for the joy you placed in my heart, the experience, and the gift of faith because if it weren't for all those things, I wouldn't be where I am with you right now. Every time I think of whom I should dedicate this book to, it goes back to you, Father God. The book that you gave me, I give it back to you from all the love that I have in my heart for you.

I also want to thank everyone that supported me and believed in me and helped me put this book together as well as those that prayed with me and for me. I asked you, in the name of Jesus, to put a special blessing upon them and their family. Thank you, Lord.

I PRAISE YOU, LORD

I praise you, Lord, for being our prince of peace; and I praise you, Lord, for being Jehovah Jireh, Jehovah Nissi, Jehovah Shalom, and Jehovah Rophe.

I praise you, Lord, for sending your son for our sins. I praise you, Lord, for providing for me, my family, and others. I praise you for protecting me, my family, and others. I praise you, Lord, because you are worthy to be praised. I praise you, Lord, because you are such an awesome God. I praise you, Lord, because there are no other gods above you. I praise you, God, for the love you place upon my heart. I praise you, God, just for you being God.

I thank you, Lord, just for waking me up in the morning. I thank you, Lord, for the family you blessed me with, and I thank you, Lord, for the books you inspired me to write. I thank you, Lord, for the patience that you have bestowed upon me. I thank you, Lord, for the challenges you have given me. I thank you, Lord, for everyone that will touch this book and receive a blessing from you, Lord—I thank you in advance for that, Lord. God, I thank you because you are the strength of my life; you are the light of my salvation. Thank you, Lord.

When the Holy Sprit inspired me to write the first book, I was trying to seek out publishers and decide on how I was going to find them. When I started out, I was looking for someone that would publish my book for me. I found several publishers, though the Holy Spirit placed in my heart that it wasn't all about the money. After being told that I quit looking for someone to publish it for me, I decided to choose a self-publisher because I knew if he said it wasn't all about the money, he would lead me in the right direction.

I knew it had to have been of God and the love I have for him for me to step out the way I did. I said I will do it again, and I am doing it again because it is all about my father and about what makes him happy. If we all learn how to be obedient to his word, I can't imagine what this world would be like. Thank you, Lord.

<<<<<<<<<<<<<<<<<<<<<<<<<<<<<<<<<<<<<<<<<<<

The Importance of Praise and Worship

One evening, there was a young lady who was going through a situation where Satan was attacking her mind. Thank God for her mother's praise and worship and for the love she has for God, Satan did not succeed. It's so important to praise and worship God all the time because when Satan tries to attack your family, your home, your friends, and even your neighbors, God knows your beginning, middle, and end. He can work things out for you before situations occur—through your praise and worship, and if you have that faith to know that he will take you through for his glory. You know that if it is for his glory, you will have a successful ending. Satan was trying to send this young lady to a state where she didn't know anyone. Satan still had her mind confused, making her think that that's where she needed to go; but thank God, through her mother's faith and prayers, she was strong enough to know what she needed to do was to pray. There were about five of us on the prayer line with her, and at one point, when she said she was going to another state, she asked me to pray and ask God what she needed to do. Right then and there, instantly, he placed in my heart, "home, home"; and before I could get the word out to tell her that the Holy Spirit said to come home, she said, "I'm coming home." "I'll let her know"—that's exactly what the Spirit told me. Now she's doing fine, she's working, and God is using her to share many blessings. She is also going to receive many blessings and favor because in spite of everything, she still believes and trusts in God. When he told her to come home, she was already going to receive favor from God.

<<<<<<<<<<<<<<<<<<<<<<<<<<<<<<<<<<<<<<<<<<<<

True Worship

When I go into praise and worship, I know I always worship God in truth because I feel him in my spirit when I worship him, not knowing I was doing what God wanted me to do. In order to be a true worshipper, you have to bow down and release everything and give it to God. You would have to give up all material things that are not of God; you have to give your children, your spouse; and you have to empty yourself to God. I know I have already done these things, and that's why when I go into worship, I can be in his glory and he will take my spirit and places where he wants it to go. That's when God truly uses me because I have no hindrance in my body. I was always wondering what was going on with me when he showed me death before it happened, when he moved my spirit from one state to another.

<<<<<<<<<<<<<<<<<<<<<<<<<<<<<<<<<<<<<<<<<<<

Woman of Faith

This great woman of God has inspired me directly and indirectly. She would often talk about faith as a requirement for God's favor. It did not matter on which occasion I decided to visit; I would always find myself in a conversation with her about God and his wonder-working power. Even though at the moment she speaks, I never let her know how many times the spirit of conviction came over me to have faith. At the time, I was attending school full-time and working full-time; my classes would start at 8:00 a.m. and end at 3:15 p.m., and then I would go to work from 4: 00 p.m. to midnight. I did that for three consecutive years. One particular day, I visited my stepmother, and I had one more year in school. I never understood how people could reach to the high point of completion and want to quit, but I was there.

I was burnt out, and I had a decision to make—quit school and continue working to pay my bills, or quit working and complete my degree requirements. I was heavy burdened, but I never stated it to her. She began to talk to me about faith without knowing I was convicted. I went home, and I read and repeated Hebrews 11:1: "Now faith is the substance of things hoped for and the evidence of things not seen." Through that conviction, I made up my mind to step out on faith. I quit my job without any cash flow coming in, and I completed school and received my degree. Right now, I stand as a living testimony that Jehovah Jireh does exist; I was able to continue paying my bills without places like payday loans and cash advances.

I thank my stepmother for allowing God to use her as the vessel to convict me to have faith, and I thank God for granting me favor because I was surrounded by so many people who were willing to help.

Pray

There was a man that I knew; he was sick for a few months. When he went back to work, one of his legs was stiff. When he walked, the leg made him walk slowly. He said he can feel the numbness in his right leg. Right then I just asked him if he knew he could be healed; he looked at me and shook his head up and down, as if he didn't know what to say. He said his sister gave him a spiritual book to read every day. He says that yes, he believes in God, but God cannot heal him from the sickness he had. I looked at him wondering, *What's wrong with him? He must not know the God that I know.* "Don't you know he has the power to heal anyone from any kind of sickness?" He just looked at me and heard the words that were flowing out of my mouth. I don't remember the words exactly, but I could tell it was the word of the Holy Spirit. When I asked him again if he wants to be healed, he told me yes, and I asked him if he would like to walk outside with me. While he was walking outside with me, he said his leg was numb and felt hot, so I looked back at him and called his name and told him he is being healed right this minute. "God is healing your leg right now." I said to him, "Let's pray." The Holy Spirit placed in my heart to tell him to walk his normal way of walking. I told him to walk his normal walk and he did. He just stepped out walking normally. I praised God for him, and I told him to thank God and praise him. I don't know what happened with his faith because he did not start out with any kind of faith, but thank God, something happened when I was talking to him. Thanks be to God. I told him he has to continue to have faith and know that God healed him. He received it, and he thanked God, and he is still walking his normal way. He started jumping in place and began laughing. It was awesome. All I did was thank God and laugh along with him. The next morning when he saw me, he said to me, "My angel," so I knew he received and he believes. *Thank you, God, for using me. I love to see people happy and not hurting.* "Of the doctrine of baptisms, and of laying on of hands, and of resurrection of the dead, and of eternal judgment. And this will we do, if God permit" (Heb. 6:2-3). *Use me, God, use me.*

<<<<<<<<<<<<<<<<<<<<<<<<<<<<<<<<<<<<<<<<<<<

Pray

A a young lady asked me to pray for her son, so I went and prayed for her family. Sometimes the Spirit will place something in my heart right away, and sometimes it takes awhile to receive a word. When he did give me a word for this family, he told me to tell the mother to plead the blood over her family. I know that normally, men are the covenant of the family, but God sees and he knows what a family needs. Also, he knows the person in the family holding the faith. When the Holy Spirit told me to tell her to plead the blood over her family, he knew Satan was out there, and he wanted to attack her family. She received the word that the Holy Spirit gave to me, knowing she would just have to walk out on faith, on his word, and start pleading the blood over her family. Once you start pleading the blood over your family, every chance you get, you can plead the blood either in the morning, afternoon, evening, or night. And anytime between those times, just plead the blood over your family. It doesn't matter if it is for finances, job problems, sickness, family dysfunction, etc. Tie it, tangle it, knot it in the blood of Jesus, and walk out in your faith, and stand and wait for the Holy Spirit to give your deliverance.

One night I was at an intercessory prayer meeting, and the minister was invited to the meeting to witness what this group was truly about, which is God's work. We introduced ourselves and told him about the intercessory prayer group. After we got through talking, he let us know he knows the true Holy Spirit of God and if someone has the true Holy Spirit. When he said that my eyes connected with his eyes, I told him I know the Spirit of God. Also, at that time, the Spirit placed in my heart that he has to let some people go because the Holy Spirit wants to use him more spiritually. When he said that to me, I just looked at him; when he has service, the Holy Spirit shows me how he glows. The minister said that he will support anyone that's walking in the Holy Spirit. At that time, the Holy Spirit, with his sweet voice, placed in my heart that the pastor would have to let some people out of his life.

I kept those words until God was ready for me to tell him; so I stood still until God said go, which was a year later. One Sunday, the minister said to the congregation that he saw a group of people dressed in white that were pushing him back and another group in white that was pushing him forward. He said the group in the back was pushing him forward and they prevailed, and the group in the front that was pushing him back failed because the power of the Holy Spirit stands against Satan. That's when the Spirit led me to the minister that Sunday to tell him what the Spirit placed in my heart a year ago, not knowing if he was going to receive me or not. To know what the Holy Spirit placed in my heart, I could stand with strength when I told him, not knowing if he received me or not, but I did what the Holy Spirit told me to do. That's the kind of love I have for my God—wherever he leads me I will go, whatever he tells me I will say. After I told him I was right, I felt the peace in my heart.

When you say yes to God and your heart and mind is open for him to lead you, you just follow him and stand in his word, and he will place in your mind, heart, and spirit that it is important to recognize his voice when the Spirit speaks to you. I heard the question once, who are you and why does the Holy Spirit speak to you? The answer for that is, the Holy Spirit wants to speak to everyone, but your heart and mind has to be open to receive him, and you also have to know how to start a relationship with God. And also, seek after his heart because he wants to have a relationship with all of us, if we just allow the door to open to our heart. When the day comes when you allow that to happen, you will never want to close the door on God ever again. However he leads you, you will do as he says because you will know the glory that he puts upon your heart. It can stand all negative because you know God will also give you his strength to stand. So whenever they look at you in a way that they think you don't know what you're talking about, continue to stand for God's glory. When you move hate, anger, and other things that you are carrying in your heart, you cannot let God in if your heart is full of things that are not of God.

God also wants his children to get to know him. That's why he tells you to come as you are; he will help you clean your heart and replace it with love because God is love. When you let God lead you, he will send you to someone that needs a word from him, and when he gives you that word, it may be for today or it may be for tomorrow. Just stand and he will give you the right way when the time is right. I said all that to say this: One night the Holy Spirit led me and another saint to go to pray for a church sister, and we did. While we were praying, the Holy Spirit placed in my heart and my spirit that he wants to give the young lady peace. I told her that the Holy Spirit wants to give her peace and that he wants her to be happy. We went to pray for one situation, but the Holy Spirit led us to pray for something else that we did not know was about to occur a couple of months later. He wanted her to stay in his will, and she would receive that peace that he had for her. She had death in her family, and whenever you have death in some families, Satan starts to come from all angles to plant negative seeds in your spirits. After the death of her family member, who was living with her for many years, other family members took over and arranged the home-going service. She was devastated because she felt excluded as they did not recognize her in any way. That's when the Holy Spirit placed in my heart that it was peace that he wanted her to have, but she will have to stay in his will to give her that peace. Every time Satan tries to step in the situation, she will have to remember what God wants for her—that's peace and to stay in God's will. When you stay in God's will, you will do what you know would make God happy. On the day of the home-going service, I must say that the Holy Spirit was in the atmosphere because she was obedient to his word, and when I spoke to her, she said she was in peace and she was happy for how everything turned out. She listened to God's word, and that's what he will do for you when you stay in his will.

God, I truly thank you for giving me the word that you placed in my spirit and you let me be able to stand and call out your word even though some did not receive it.

Though the person it's intended for received it. Thank God, because if she did not receive it, Satan would have succeeded in planting his negative seed.

I was studying the book of Daniel three to four weeks, and at the fourth week, I was going in the book of Proverbs, but the spirit led me back to the book of Daniel for seven more days. I know there was a reason why he led me back to the book of Daniel. During that same week, there was a friend that came to me at work, and we talked. She told me her ankle was swollen. She told me to pray for her ankle later that day. At the same time, the Spirit placed in my heart to pray for her right then. Suddenly, I put my right hand around her ankle because my hand was getting heavy and it seemed like electricity was running through my arms, and I said a prayer. After the prayer, I told her it was done, and the rest was up to her; her faith would have to allow her to receive the healing that the Holy Spirit granted. With all the experience I had, that was the first time I had 100 percent faith, plus knowing that the Holy Spirit was using me for his vessel. It was a good feeling knowing that the Holy Spirit was doing the work and that I was the body being used for his glory. It's an awesome feeling to have that kind of faith to know that the Holy Spirit is healing others through your body. Now when someone asks me to pray, it's not a scary feeling running through my body anymore; I can stand on the highest faith there is because I know God is doing all the work, not me. When a person comes with the highest faith, they will be healed by the Holy Spirit. There are many different types of healing, and the Holy Spirit will lead you to the kind of healing the person is supposed to get even though it's not explained to you at the time. When someone tells you, you have to have faith as small as a mustard seed, just remember it takes more than a mustard seed faith to handle large situations. You want to grow tall as large trees, as wide as the sea—that's when you can taste the faith that you have and you can walk in his glory. It's also great to know that you have that kind of relationship with the Holy Spirit that you can give him back his word that he gave you. And I'm not talking about the words in the Bible, I'm talking about when he said all I have to do is lay hands, pray, and he will take over from there; that's why he's such an awesome man to love because he keeps his word. When my friend walked away, she walked away with no pain. Later that week, I asked her about her healing, and she said she thanked God for the healing he gave her. That's why when I was reading the book of Daniel, my faith was growing while I was reading. The experience in the book of Daniel 3:20, 25, 26 is about Shadrach, Meshach, Abednego, and the amount of faith they had to know that God would save them out of the fiery furnace. I have experienced a hot furnace also, which was a part of my job when I was a welder. It was a hot experience working in the furnace, which was cut off and the fire covered with cores. So I knew that if the furnace is high and on, you have to have some awesome faith and trust in God to know that he is going to deliver you out of a place like that.

Father God, I praise you for how you can bring the past, present, and future, and make it one, Father God, how you direct lives so they can have the opportunity to know who you're really all about. They can keep their eyes on you and stay in your will; there is so much to know about God. *God, to know you is to love you.* And I am going to tell you how God directed this young man's life at this time. This young man loves sports; his dream was to play in the NFL, and he was looking forward to playing. A man assured him that he was going to make it to the NFL; but it was a turnaround—it didn't work out for him, his spirit was broken, and he felt like he was let down because of the promise, and he knew he was an awesome player. Knowing how much he loved this sport, it hurts me knowing that he was hurting. That Monday when I went to work, I had a pain of burden down in my stomach, and it lasted all day. When I got home from work, I cried out in pain to God to let him know that I was not hurting for myself; the pain I was carrying was for the young man. I was asking God to give him a break, though, and grant him his favor. He gave me peace about him. Later on that night, two different families heard on the evening news that he was going to the NFL. It seems weird, but that's what happened. I know God was involved because he always gives me peace about his situation when I prayed for him. In my spirit, I knew something good was going to happen for him; I just didn't know what. I know he believes in God and trusts in God. Not knowing that God had other plans for him, something he was already being trained for by playing the sport he loved. Instead of being an NFL player, he was given the opportunity to be a coach for one of the largest universities in the east. He thinks that God went to sleep on him, not knowing God had his eyes on him all the time. God wanted him to know that "when you're at your lowest point, you might not feel me, but knowing that I'm there and I have my arms around you to tell you it is going to be all right, I will take care of you. Hear me, I will take care of you; your spirit will be broken a little now, but you will love me more later, my son. Thank you for listening to my words when you were hurting; thank you for listening to my words when you were feeling all alone. Thank you for calling out my name whenever you thought I forsake you. Thank you because you know that I am real."

<<<<<<<<<<<<<<<<<<<<<<<<<<<<<<<<<<<<<<<<<<<<

Forgive Me, Lord

Peace I will give you, so don't let your heart be troubled. I know this young man, and once upon a time, he broke one of the commandments.

One morning when this event supposedly had happened, he told me it was someone else. In my spirit, it didn't seem right, but I went in to pray, knowing what happened shouldn't have happened; so I was praying for the persons involved, but the Holy Spirit led me into a prayer that wouldn't affect anyone. And at the same time, he placed in my spirit that the young man was not telling me the truth, but I had no words to say to him about the situation because the young man I'm talking about is my son. That's why the Holy Spirit allowed me to pray that way because if I had prayed harm, it would have fallen on him. In any prayer, the Holy Spirit takes over your prayer and guides you how to pray; he always knows the situation you're praying about because you really don't know that's why he guides you, and I thank God for that. It was years after that happened that my son was telling me about all the bills and the situation that he was in. It seems like every time he gets up, Satan tries to attack him with something else. That day we were talking, I went to pray to talk to God about my son's situation, and he placed in my heart that he needs to ask God for forgiveness for what he did. A couple of days later, I told him what the Holy Spirit said to me, and he said that yes, he will. A week or two later, he had jobs coming toward him, offering more than what he was making on his permanent job; they were coming to him to ask him to work for them. I asked him if he knew that was God granting him favor, that that's God who wants us to recognize when were wrong, ask for forgiveness, and be sincere. He recognized that was God working for him. He asked me how I knew it was him, and I told him the about the Holy Spirit and how he directed my pray, and when "I knew it was you. That's why you have to stay in constant prayer for your children, friends, family, and loved ones. God wants to be there for everyone who recognizes that he is real. He is still alive, and he is with us every minute of the day." Thank you, Lord.

<<<<<<<<<<<<<<<<<<<<<<<<<<<<<<<<<<<<<<<<<<<

Vision, Dreams, Faith

One night, my intercessory prayer group and I were in prayer, and the Holy Spirit was so high in the room. I was in prayer when the Holy Spirit showed me a vision of Moses and Abraham. It was like in a circle. The first face I saw was Abraham; he placed in my heart, Abraham; then Moses's face appeared to me, and the Spirit placed in my heart Moses's name. Even though I saw the faces, I would not know it was Abraham or Moses. By that note, those men had different callings. So God shows us in dreams and visions. He speaks to us, and he trains us for our calling. Once God appoints you for your calling, no one can work your calling but you. For instance, Dr. Martin Luther King had a calling in his life. I never realized that he was a man of God, and he stood up with Abraham and Moses. That's why Dr. Martin Luther King was never afraid of the challenge that was ahead of him because he knew God had assured him and had given him that peace and joy to do what God wanted him to do. He trusted God to know that his family was not going to be hurt. That's why when they threw bombs in his house and when he was stabbed—a breath away from death—God had him covered for such a time like that. Once God places peace and once you know he's leading you, he directs your path for whatever he wants you to do. No one can tell you not to do something because God already placed it in your spirit. And Dr. Martin Luther King's calling was to initiate the civil rights movement. That's why no one could pick up the torch after he died because God had anointed him, and no one else, for that calling. I thanked God for putting that in my spirit because I would not dream I would be writing this about Dr. Martin Luther King; I never thought about him that way. I never looked at him as one of God's special men like Moses and Abraham until the Holy Spirit placed it in my heart, right this minute while I'm writing. What a revelation it was when I saw a minister preaching some of the same things about this anointed man on TBN; he placed him up there with God's anointed. I know it was so awesome when I heard him preaching about Dr. Martin Luther King. I wasn't sure if it was right for me to write this or not, but after I heard the preacher, it was a confirmation of what the Spirit had placed in my heart about him. It seemed as if I could feel the Spirit when I was writing. In order for him to succeed in his calling—and as righteous as he was—he had to have the kind of faith that you would find in these scriptures:

> By faith Abraham, when he was called to go out into a place which he should after receive for an inheritance, obeyed; and he went out, not knowing whither he went (Heb. 11:8).

> Now faith is the substance of things hoped for, the evidence of things not seen (Heb. 11:1).

> Through faith we understand that the worlds were framed by the word of God, so that things which are seen were not made of things which do appear (Heb. 11:3).

<<<<<<<<<<<<<<<<<<<<<<<<<<<<<<<<<<<<<<<<<<<

Dream

One Friday night, the Holy Spirit showed me where I met a man, and he was telling me about how much he loves God; and he told me there was a place that he wanted to show me because he built it because he loved God just that much. He took me to a place that looked like a desert. He took me in a building that was underground; he showed me around and said, "I did this for God because I love him that much." The place looked just like during biblical times; and after he showed me around the place, he sat down. He was sitting on the right side of the room, and another lady was sitting near him. The man was sitting by the window. He asked the young lady what was her calling, and nothing came out of her mouth. I raised my hand and said I was writing a book, and I didn't say anymore. The voice of a spirit came out and said he inspired me to write books 1and 2 because he knows how much I love God. I stood up not realizing I was standing in front of the window; I felt an awesome wind blow in my face. I was looking at the window; I didn't understand where the wind was coming from because the curtain was blowing from the wind that was blowing upon my body. I was looking for a fan, but I did not see one. I knew the wind that was blowing did not feel like an air conditioner; I just did not understand at first because the building was underground, and the wind could not blow underground. The Spirit placed in my heart to let me know that it was neither a fan nor an air conditioner; he let me know it was the breath from the Holy Spirit. "And when the day of Pentecost was fully come, they were all with one accord in one place. And suddenly there came a sound from heaven as of a rushing mighty wind, and it filled all the house where they were sitting" (Acts 2:1-2). I walked toward the man, and it was beautiful noise upstairs. I asked him if he has children, and he did not answer. I looked around toward the door, and I looked at how the door was made; saints could walk in and out whenever they wanted to because that place was on holy ground, and the room that I asked him about upstairs was placed in my heart—it was the upper room. That's why your dreams tell you a lot; it shows you where you're at with God. It is important to be able to identify your dreams; if it is of God you will know, and if it is of Satan you will know also because Satan will always try to steal your joy and your peace away.

One morning before I left for work, the Holy Spirit placed in my heart that I will be praying with a young lady I know. Later that day, I saw the young lady, and she was upset. She was telling me that her mother went to the hospital the day before and that she found out she had cancer, and she was telling me about her condition. I listened, though I had nothing to say at the time. Then I remembered the Holy Spirit told me we were going to pray that day. I called her out by her name, and I let her know that the Holy Spirit had already let me know we were going to pray that day. I was praying for her mother, and I was praying in the Spirit for her mother; and the Holy Spirit placed in my heart the word through it all. And in my spirit, he let me know he was in the hospital room that very second with her mother. The word that he gave me and also put into my spirit was, he will be there with her through all she has to endure. Because of the faith she had in God and belief the God was going to be with her through it all, she knew her time was limited, she did not stop one day to give herself a pity party. She kept on doing what she would always do on her normal day activities; she took herself to the doctor to receive her chemotherapy and any other appointments. She did whatever she felt like doing. She even had the strength to help arrange her funeral; she told everyone what she wanted them to do that day of her home-going service. The day she was here, about midday, she was on her journey; her daughter and I was at a shop together, and there was a strong odor of perfume that passed through us. It was a strong scent; no one was around, and neither of us had that type of perfume on. I asked her daughter if she smelled it. Neither one of us realized what was happening, and the next morning her daughter called me and told me that that scent of perfume was her mother's because her mother died about four hours later after we smelled the scent. When you have that kind of faith, and you don't lose it when you hear bad news, and you stay in God's will, he will give you peace until the end and the strength that you need to go through it all. He will walk with you hand in hand. When he gave me the word for her, he will be there through it all; God sure was there with her through it all. God loves his children just that much; that's why he said, "I will never leave you nor forsake you."

Thank you, Lord.

There was a man whom I knew; I never see him that often, maybe once in a while in church. I would pass his house sometimes when I'm on my way from work, and every time I pass his house it would leave a burden in my heart. I would say that his house needs to be worked on because I see some things that I wouldn't mind fixing, and I thought that was the burden that was lying in my heart. I would pass it about four or more times, and I still feel the same burden; I took it to my prayer group, and I mentioned it to others about that burden I had about his house. One night, the Holy Spirit had me prophesize to myself that if the first book makes any money, his house will be the first house I will work on. The Holy Spirit also placed in my heart that if his house isn't there, I would work on another house. But why would I say that if his house isn't there, I would work on another house? Personally, I feel his house would always be there, but the next day when I got home from work, I did not drive pass his house. When I got home, I was told that the man died in a house fire. So when I was thinking God wanted me to work on his house, God actually wanted me to go in his house to work on his soul. See, God wants all his children with him. I did not make it there, but I know God sent someone else for his glory because he knows I didn't understand what he wanted me to do at that time. I know that God truly wanted me to see so I would know what to do if it happens again. That's how God trains us for such a time as this; that's why we need to have "patience, experience, and hope" (Rom. 5:4). There are a lot of believers and nonbelievers that don't believe the gift that God give us in healing, prophesizing, soul healing, and deliverance; they believe it happened in the old and new testaments, but they don't believe it happens in everyday life. "Now it was not written for his sake alone, that it was imputed to him; But for us also, to whom it shall be imputed, if we believe on him that raised up Jesus our Lord from the dead" (Rom. 4:23-24).

God showed me in a dream that I was standing on the side of the road, and it looked like Jesus was in front of a crowd witnessing. Right then and there, the Holy Spirit placed in my heart that I was one of Jesus's followers. That's why I said to my God that yes, I just want to be about God's business and nothing else. It is an awesome feeling to feel the Holy Spirit working on my soul and my mind. It is hard to describe to anyone who's not really at that level with God because they hear you, and at the same time, they don't hear you. That's why it's so hard to look at believers and see how they treat others; and they will say that they don't believe in prophets, and they don't believe that the Holy Spirit speaks to you, and they don't believe in true healing. Yet still they will say they are children of God. That's when you know for yourself that they can't be of God because God doesn't have his believers to respond to anyone in a disrespectful manner because God only comes with positive; he takes you higher. And he wants everyone who's connected to him only to speak positive because of the powers in your tongue—the power of life and death, good and bad. God is not a respecter of persons, and he loves us all.

One Thursday night, I was lying in my bed; and I was thinking about all the things that are happening in the world—the killings and other crimes, and how Satan is attacking the minds of the young people, and also, there were some people with whom I was talking to who were having the same problem with the mind. While I was lying in my bed, it laid a burden upon my heart, and I started thinking about my daughter and how the intercessors need to go out and pray for the young people in the world. I got out of my bed, and I said to my daughter, "Do you know sometimes you can hear other voices that tell you to do things that do not match your heart and are not of God?" Her response to me was that it happened to her in class; she told me that something in her head told her to pick up a chair and hit another classmate with it because they had exchanged words in class. At that time,

I thanked God for his grace and mercy, and I thanked God for teaching me how to pray and to go into worship for such a time like this. I asked her if she liked to be angry, and she said no; I asked her if she wanted help, and she said yes. And I was not talking about medication; I was talking about Dr. Jesus. I thanked God that she recognized that God was there with her to prevent something serious from happening, and we went into prayer and asked God to remove the spirit of anger and give her the spirit of patience. I just pray that she received it and keep the faith that God will be there in any situation if she allows him to be there in the future for her.

God, I thank you, in the name of Jesus, for being there for my daughter when she walked in the situation she was in, and I love you even more; thank you, Lord.

One day I was in my car, and the Holy Spirit placed in me a spiritual reader; at first when he placed that in my heart, it made me think about psychics and palm readers, and I said to God, "Did you place this in my heart because I don't want to do nothing if it's not of you?" It was bounding in my heart—spiritual reading, spiritual reading, spiritual reading—letting me know that it's of God. And to confirm it for me, I got a revelation from Benning Hynns when he was talking about the issue of blood; when the woman touched Jesus and he asked the question who touched him, he was not talking about his garment, he was talking about her faith. And her spirit touched his spirit; both spirits met. That's when it took me back to when I was talking to a young lady about her father; and after we got through talking, I embraced her, and by embracing her, the Spirit let me know that he wanted to use her father for his glory. Once I touched an obituary, and the Spirit let me know that her spirit was of God. There are a lot of other things my spirit showed me, where I can stand in one place and my spirit can go to another place. For example, I was praying for a young lady, and my spirit went to her bedroom; and when I saw her sister, I told her I was at her house that morning, not realizing what I was saying, not knowing that God was showing me there was another gift he was allowing me to use. Whenever I go into prayer for someone, it is a deep prayer; I go into by putting my whole body, soul, and mind into the prayer. That's why whenever God tells you about a gift that you are using such as spiritual reader, I was being trained to see if I would pass every test that he gave to me to see if I would stand and be obedient and trust that he was leading me. When he said spiritual reading, he was confirming something that I was doing all the time; he just let me know that what I was doing has a name. It makes you feel strange when something new happens; it makes you wonder what's going on. When you say yes to God, you will have new callings and challenges as long as you stay in God's will and be obedient to his direction.

Thank you, God, for trusting me and teaching me your way, I will not have it any other way because what it takes for me to make it in heaven, I will do it with an open heart. Thank you, Lord.

<<<<<<<<<<<<<<<<<<<<<<<<<<<<<<<<<<<<<<<<<<<<<<<<

Love

God is love. Sometimes you think people don't receive you when you tell someone that you just met you love them. They might think you're saying that because it's a word. But when you receive God and you're a true Christian, and once God places that joy in your heart and you love God in a way that makes your heart melt just by thinking about him, you are truly of God; you can truly love any and everyone in spite of. There was one time I went to a funeral where a mother had lost her son. She was hurting, and by that note, I told her what I was feeling when I embraced her; and I told her that I loved her. No, I didn't know her, but I did have love in my heart for her because of the connection that I have with God. At first when I heard about her son, I prayed and asked God what do I say to someone that lost a child to a violent act? He placed in my heart that he is also a mother's child too. After the funeral, the mother stated that she did not understand how people in general can come up to her and tell her they love her, but when someone of God comes to you and say they love you, it is not them themselves, it is the Holy Spirit within them. That when God puts that joy of love in your spirit to release to someone that is hurting or in need of an encouraging word at that time, it is not the person themselves saying it, it is the Holy Spirit speaking through them. If God is in you and Jesus is in God and God is in Jesus—with that mixture—nothing but the love of Jesus should come out of you. You will say I love you whether you want to say it or not. You will feel it in your spirit whether you want to or not because once you receive God, the Holy Spirit, you receive God's love. When I see someone mistreat or break someone's spirit and they don't do anything to correct it, it makes me wonder if they truly know God and his ways. That's why if you truly have a relationship with God and you actually love God the way you are supposed to, you would know when you do something that is not of God. If he does not disturb your spirit, you do not have that relationship you say you have. He wants you to love each and every one of his children. He is not a sometime God, he is an all-time God. He wants us to be the same way; he wants us to reach out to our sisters and brothers so their souls can be saved, so they can have a chance when their time expires, and so they will also have a place in heaven. He doesn't want you to do anything to break his children's spirit because he loves each and every one of us, not just because we are Christians and not just because we are in a church. One can be in jail, living on the street, have any kind of bad habits, and he still loves them just as much as he loves you. That's why we have Christians; there is a joy that he puts in our hearts that we can explain. He gives you that kind of joy and love so you can be able to communicate and reach God's loved ones' heart. Such as this, this is a young lady that I have never met; we have only talked on the phone to each other, and at this time I would like you to review a letter of appreciation. If you should read this book, I would like if you would get in touch with me; yes, I still love you in the name of Jesus, and you will still stay in my prayers.

Thank you so much for spending some of your time with me today. I'm so glad you remembered me and included me in your prayers, and most of all, thank you for loving me despite the fact that we're too far from each other. I never expected us to go this far. I thought you were just someone who I'd get to talk to at some point in time, but I know God planned all this, and we reached this far. You have taught me a lot and made me learn a lot of things that I didn't know would be possible. Your faith, your words, and you made me realize that I am special and loved. And right now, I feel so good to know that somebody out there loves me, and I know this person really loves me because I can feel it! You made me realize that no matter what's going to happen to me, no matter how rough my life could be, God is there and will be there for me, so I've got to have faith and strength to stand. In the past few days, I've been so frustrated, discontented, a failure, ahh! I felt all those. I'm the kind of person that easily gets sick when a problem arises. I'm having the hardest time dealing with tough situations, but I thank you because you came to my rescue. Words are not enough to express my gratitude. If you could read what's written in my heart right now—you could see the longing for God, your words, gratitude, joy. And you did all these. Thank you for loving me. I pray we will remain in each other's hearts forever.

I met a man at a social gathering, and the first time I saw him I could see that he had connection with the Holy Spirit, and he was a child of God. I looked at him, and I never said anything to him other than greeting him. One morning he had a meeting with a group of us, and he was telling the group about himself and what he expects out of the group and what the group should expect from him. After he got through introducing himself to the group and we were dismissed, I still did not say anything to him, and I walked out of the room. My first thought was that man must have just read the book of Proverbs because everything he said lined up with the book of Proverbs. That goes to show you that if you are of God, you don't need a Bible in your hand to show that you are of God; all you have to do is live the way God would live, and you will be the walking Bible. He confirmed what God placed in my heart at one time; God wants his word planted in you, so when you meet someone burdened, if they need a word, the words will come out of you and everything you say will be contained in the Bible and in God's will. That's how you can reach people better. We never communicated after that day, but a week later, I saw him and I asked him if he was a Christian; and when I asked him, he said yes, and the look on his face was a look that let me know he was in love with God without him telling me. After he told me how good God is to him, and how much he trust and love the Lord, and the joy that showed on his face, I said to myself, "My God, this man seems like he loves God more than I do." From that day forward, whenever we talked, he would show and tell the love he had for God, and he would do whatever God wants him to do or however he directs his life. God placed in my spirit that he had something awesome for him to do, and he had many more blessings for him if he just stayed in his will. One day I was at home, he placed in my heart that he will be in ministry. The next day when I saw him, I didn't know how I was going to ask him, but I did ask if he ever thought about ministry; and he looked at me with that godly smile and he said yes and smiled and said it was placed in his heart also. A week later, he approached me because it was a burden on him; when you have a burden on doing God's work, you have to do it because that's what God wants you to do. He asked me to pray about the situation, and I did; and the Holy Spirit placed in my heart, ministry. What's so awesome was that when I told him about what was placed in my heart about the ministry school, he said he called his sister; and his sister knew what he was going to say to her, and he told her he was thinking about being a minister. I'm not sure what words he said to her, but it was in that context, and she told him she knew what he was going to tell her. She told him he needed to get more in the word of ministry. When he told me that, it gave my body a chill because I knew God was right in the middle of what was going on. He does not use one person to put a puzzle together; he uses whomever he needs to get that puzzle right.

<<<<<<<<<<<<<<<<<<<<<<<<<<<<<<<<<<<<<<<<<<<<<<<

The Prayer Shawl

I was at a family gathering, and we were talking about how good God was and also about praying. The Holy Spirit placed on one of the young lady's heart that when I go to pray, I should use a prayer shawl. I thought about it at that time that I was going to get one, but after that day, I forgot about it. Later I met this woman that makes prayer shawls, and when I saw it, it took me back to the time when the young lady told me what was placed in her heart. Right there and then, it seemed like I needed to get a shawl right away. I asked her the price, and if she would be able to make one for me. When she told me the price, I did not care about the price; I knew I needed to have one. With that price, I knew it was of God because I would have never paid for it if I was thinking about myself. I went into prayer anyway, and I asked God if it was him that wanted me to have a prayer shawl. He gave me a vision where I saw myself wrapped in a prayer shawl, and he also placed in my heart to pray over it three different times once I receive it. It seemed like I had about three weeks to a month before I had my first prayer over it. The second time I prayed over it, he set that time up also; and the last prayer I said to myself, "I'm going to pray over it tonight." And I changed my mind, and it seemed like the Holy Spirit wanted me to pray over it that particular night. After I got through praying over it, I unwrapped it and I put it over my head. The power of the Holy Spirit was so heavy that it actually scared me and I took it off, but it was a good feeling. I knew it was God that led me to have a prayer shawl. The next week, I heard Benny Hinn and someone talking about the prayer shawl, and about how it's important to use it because a prayer shawl represents being wrapped in the body of Christ. Sometimes when I go into a series of prayer, I will use my prayer shawl.

One Friday night I went into prayer with my intercessory prayer group for a minister; she was burdened by the confusion in the church and by how the members treated her and talked to her. You would think they were talking to someone that is not worth talking to. Some of the things that they said, usually if anyone realizes the words that they say to someone that breaks their spirit, they would apologize just to stay in God's will, but they did not. We went into prayer for the minister, and the Holy Spirit placed in my heart to tell her to give her back her words because her words are God words and God's words are her words. When things start coming to an end, I gave her the word God gave me to give her. At that time she wasn't listening because she was at the grieving stage as she couldn't believe the people she thought was for her were wolves in sheep's clothing. They started revealing their true form. Not surprising for me because the Holy Spirit had placed in my heart that people in the church will be revealed if they're not of God, and the ones of God will be revealed also. The Holy Spirit placed in my heart that she has to release some people because God wanted to use her, and he can't use her because she is connected to those people. It seems like everything is coming to pass; those things were placed in my heart about two years ago. And it's just now coming to pass. The minister saw the dream herself of what was now happening also, but in the dream, it will be victory if she stands and stays in God's will. I thank God for using me the way he does because when events happen that he has already placed in my heart, it is so good because I have no other choice but to stay in his will to glorify his name. It makes me even stronger, and I love God even more because every time I repeat what he says to me, it makes me stronger. I can stand with God's strength regardless of whether anyone believes me or not; I still can stand because I know what my God said to me. That Sunday, there was a minister giving the word for morning service. Everything that he was saying was as if God was giving him those words for the other minister because he was saying all the words that she needed to hear. After the service, she let the congregation know that she will no longer be with the church, and she thanked the congregation for everything they did for her and her family, but she can no longer stay there because the direction it is going is not of God. He asked three questions: Does anyone believe that God will fight your battle? Does anyone believe that God said, don't touch my anointed or do my prophet no harm? Does anyone believe that God will move your stumbling blocks? He also said that he received one of the words that the minister said: "Weeping may endure for a night, but sweet joy comes in the morning." All the words are God's words, so all he has to do is stand with God's word because if he stays in God's words, he will stay in God's will. And by staying in God's will, God will do all those things that he says because God does take care of his own. And when I say his own, anyone of us can be God's own. Just give yourself to God, and he will be your protector and provider for whichever situation you need him for. The following Tuesday, there was a congregational meeting, and in this meeting most of the church members were upset because of the way the minister was being treated. They felt that was the reason why he left. That Tuesday morning on my way to work, I was praying for peace in the meeting, and while praying, the Holy Spirit placed in my heart that no one would say a word, just be humble as a child. When the Spirit gave me those words and he directed me to call a couple of people, I told them what the Holy Spirit said to me, and they received the word and said they will be obedient to God. On my way walking into the place, the Holy Spirit placed in my heart that he will have someone doing the talking, and then I understood what he was saying to me by telling those few people to be quiet and just stand and pray. So that night, the church was full of members who wanted to know what happened, and why did the pastor leave, and why did they talk to him the way they did in the meetings? There were really no questions answered by the leaders in the church other than them saying nothing happened, not knowing that they broke his spirit by the words they were saying to him. Believe it or not, this particular meeting was shown to me two weeks before New Year's Eve; and this is August, so you can believe it, or not. But God knows what's going to happen, so you have time to change your ways and walk in his will and let him lead you in his will. God loves each and every one of us; he loves the ungodly just as well as the godly. He wants each and every one to open their hearts and get to know him and know what to do in every situation if you say that you are of God. When you do get in situations and wonder how to treat someone, just say to yourself what would God do, and then you will know how to treat and talk to your brothers and sisters in Christ. Just to know what God would do. I will now tell you about this dream I had. I did not plan to write this in this book, but when God placed it in my heart to write it, I never questioned him about a story to write that he gave me. Though this one, I thought that he would not allow me to put in this book because everything that he gives me he doesn't inspire me to put it in, so when he continued to burden my heart to put this in the book, I kept asking God, "Do you really want me to put this in the book?" I asked over and over again, and this is the title that he gave me to write this dream under because this is not my book, this is God's book. It's not about what I think is appropriate, or what I do not think is appropriate. In so many words God was saying to me, God inspired me to write this book, not Angie inspired God.

<<<<<<<<<<<<<<<<<<<<<<<<<<<<<<<<<<<<<<<<<<

I Know the Heart of the Ungodly and the Godly

It was one evening and it seemed like we were in a meeting because of the way how everyone was dressed. A minister was sitting in the pulpit, and the minister stood up and got down out of the pulpit and turned toward the pulpit. He began speaking words, but I could not hear what was being said. While I was looking at the minister, the minister was fully dressed; but while I was looking in the spiritual eyes, I saw the minister's nakedness. At first I did not understand what I was seeing when I saw the minister's nakedness. Therefore, at that time, I thought everyone in the church saw the minister's nakedness too, but I was the only one that saw the minister. After the minister finished speaking, the minister got back into the pulpit and sat down. Then the minister's spouse got up, and the spouse was saying words; but I didn't hear or understand what was being said. For some reason I got up, and I sat in a chair in the middle between the pulpit and the pews on the right side of the church. I sat there, and I looked in the minister's direction without looking in the minister's face because I was embarrassed because I knew the minister knew what I saw. The minister did not look at me. He avoided looking in my direction. Then I looked behind me at the pews, and a lot of people had left. Some were standing on the outside looking in. I got up and went back and sat by a saint and I said, "The sisters and brothers that walked out, you can tell they are not of God. All they had to do is stay and pray for the situation that is going on in the church because we all know that a family that prays together stays together."

This is the dream that God showed me, and he showed me before these things happened. That's why when I saw this dream, I kept asking saints who know how to interpret dreams about what I was seeing because I know this was a powerful dream, and it was telling me something that was going to happen. Everything that he said to me is truly coming to pass and not only in this church. I'm hearing that it's happening in other churches that people are being revealed for who they are when it comes to God. Saints and God are tired of us playing church, and he wants us to be real with our Lord. He wants us to open our hearts, minds, and souls; and he wants to pour that liquid love that he wants us to share with each other and everyone even though there were people revealed who really don't know God. To know God, you will stay in his will; and you will not do anything to move out of his will because once you are touched by his love, his anointing, and his Holy Spirit, you will not want to do nothing that is not of God. God is not a God of confusion and breaking spirits; he just wants peace, love, happiness, and joy for all his children. He loves us in spite of what we do. He's just that kind of God, so if you say God is in you and you are in God and God is in Jesus, tell me how you are supposed to represent God. That is love because that is what God is.

I prayed and asked God what I should do in this situation that's going on. I prayed and I talked to God, and I asked God why he is not placing words in my heart to tell me what I need to do. Do I need to stay in this church? Why aren't you putting it in my spirit what I should do? I can't understand how you would keep me in a church with so many ungodly leaders. God placed nothing in my heart to stay.

God, I just don't understand, but I know you told me to stand, and I know you said to pray. But every time I prayed about this situation about this minister, you always placed in my heart his dream.

And his dream was that there was a group of people in white. The large group of people in white was behind him, and a small group of people in white was in front of him. The ones that were in front of him were pushing him back, and the group in the back was pushing him forward and was telling him to continue moving forward. He said the group in the back pushed him on through, and there was victory for him. He also placed in my heart when he told me he wanted to use the pastor much higher than he is now to do his work, but he has to release some people. I don't know who the people are, but he placed it in my heart, and the people will be revealed just because they don't know him. God doesn't want all-weather Christians. He wants everyday Christians that love him and that want to get to know him and that have an everyday relationship with him and also a personal relationship. If you have all these things, you got God and you know him; you don't have to pretend because that is hard work. The easy way out is to have faith in knowing how real God is. Just stand for God because if you stand for God, you stand for truth.

<<<<<<<<<<<<<<<<<<<<<<<<<<<<<<<<<<<<<<<<<<<<<<<

Pray

One night I was praying for my church family, and while I was praying, the Holy Spirit placed in my heart to call out cancer. At that time, I didn't know what body I was calling cancer out of, but I was obedient and continued calling cancer out. You see when you pray and you are truly of God, he will lead your prayer in a prayer for someone else rather you knowing what's going on or not. About a month after that, I was told that this saint had cancer. God continued to lead me into prayer for this saint constantly. It felt just like a burden if I did not pray for this saint. While I was praying, God gave me peace about the situation. When I found out that God had healed this saint because of the faith that the saint had, I knew and believed by any shadow of a doubt that God was going to heal this saint, and this saint was healed. Thank God for the saint's obedience to his words.

Thank you, God, for being the dependable God that you are, and it is so awesome to know that God can be so dependable. Thank you, God, for being the saint's doctor. Thank you, God, for being the saint's medicine. Thank you, God, for embracing when you are needed. Thank you, God, for being you; and you are worthy to be loved.

There was a young man that had a stiff neck and a headache, and his mom was telling him to come to my house so I can pray and lay hands on him; but he said that he was not able to come because it was hurting badly. At the time, we were telling him that in order for it to work, he had to have faith that God was using me for his vessel and he had to have faith to know that God will heal him. At that time, we both felt like he did not believe that God is in the healing power. A week later I talked with him on the phone, and he asked me if I prayed for him that night because when he woke up he had no pain; and he told me that he knew I was going to pray for him. And by that note, just him knowing that I was going to pray to God for him, God healed him because he did have faith to know that God has the power to heal. *Thank you, Lord, for showing him that you are God.* See what can you do to have the power in your tongue; I don't think he realized the power he had, that's why you have to be careful what you say because the power of life and death is in the words that come out of your mouth. Whatever you speak positive it will be positive when it comes to God.

　　Thank you, God, for being there for him just to realize that you are a man of your words and if you believe in God and how real he is.

Do I Know God?

God, when I go to church I sit beside my neighbor, and I turn my head and don't say good morning, do I know you, Lord? When a drug dealer, drug user, and prostitute come to church to turn their lives around and turn their lives over to God, and I shut the door in there face, do I know you, Lord? When the minister is giving his word for the day, and I shut his word out of my heart and don't receive that word that he is giving me, do I know you, Lord? When I talk to saints and say what I want to say, and it doesn't matter if I break their spirit or not, do I know you, Lord? Lord, when I can tell the untruth about my sisters and brothers and it doesn't matter to me, do I know you, Lord? When I just want to do things my way if it's fair or not as a leader and don't do my part as a leader, do I know you, Lord? These are just small things that I am doing, do I know you, Lord? Lord, you say you can give me peace and joy, Lord, so why am I like this, Lord; why am I carrying these thing in my heart? Please change me, Lord; I'm crying out for your love so I can be free from all these sins that are in my heart, Lord, but, Lord, these are still small things. But do I know you, Lord? Lord, they say all I have to do is believe that you are real and Jesus died for our sins, and he is your only son, Lord, do I know you, Lord? No one taught me how to live your way, Lord; no one taught me how to walk in your will, do I know you, Lord? Lord, I was told all I have to do is believe that you are real, do I know you, Lord? God, they say you do not speak to anyone anymore; you stopped speaking in the Old Testament in the Bible, do I know you, Lord? But, God, why do we have teachers in the churches that teach your word, but they don't obey your words? Because they don't know you, Lord! But, God, you say the word is God's word and the word is God, do I know you, Lord? God, I want you to heal my sins, my heart, my soul, my mind, and my flesh. Do I know you, Lord? Lord, I ask you in the name of Jesus, I ask you to transform my mind in your will mold my heart in your will; I want to know you, Lord! Lord, teach me how to have this personal relationship with you. Lord, I want to know you, Lord!

II Peter 1:6-10

6   And to knowledge temperance; and to temperance patience; and to patience godliness;
7   And to godliness brotherly kindness; and to brotherly kindness charity.
8   For if these things be in you, and abound, they make you that ye shall neither be barren nor unfruitful in the knowledge of our Lord Jesus Christ.
9   But he that lacketh these things is blind, and cannot see afar off, and hath forgotten that he was purged from his old sins.
10 Wherefore the rather, brethren, give diligence to make your calling and election sure: for if ye do these things, ye shall never fall.

And thank you, Lord, for giving me the gift of faith, and that's why you are so worthy to be praised.

<<<<<<<<<<<<<<<<<<<<<<<<<<<<<<<<<<<<<<<<<<<<<<<<<

I Want to Please You, Lord

Lord, I want you to get deeper in me, Lord, so I can stay in your will just to please you, Lord. Lord, I want you to take what's in me that's not of you so I can walk in your will, Lord, just to please you, Lord! Lord, I want you to teach me how to love and pray for my enemies and all the saints just to please you, Lord! Lord, I just want you to pour your love in my heart so I can give it back to others just to please you, Lord. Lord, I want you to go in the deepest part of my mind, soul, and body. Wash me clean with hyssop and blunt all my sins just to please you, Lord. Lord, I just want to pour all my love on you, Lord; I just want to stay in your presence and glorify your name and most of all, stay in your glory. And I just want to say yes, yes, yes, Lord, just use me for your vessel just to please you, Lord. Lord, I just want to give my body back to you as a living sacrifice; I just want to walk, sleep, think, smile, and laugh in your will, Lord, just to please you, Lord. Lead me, Lord, so I can stay in your will until you call me home, Lord. The love that I have for you, I can taste it in my soul that's why I want to please you, Lord. Lord, you make my night turn into light, you make my storm turn into joy, you make my hate turn into love just to please you, Lord. I love you; thank you in the name of Jesus. You are my everything. I love to praise you, Lord.

<<<<<<<<<<<<<<<<<<<<<<<<<<<<<<<<<<<<<<<<<<<<<<

Lead Me, Lord

Every morning before I go to work, I would sit in my car and pray; and when I get through praying, I will ask God in Jesus's name, "Do not let no weapon form against me prosper, and don't let no tongues come against me!" And before the day is out, here are couple of things that had happened: First, there was a young lady that I knew; she asked a few people a couple things about me, which she already knew the answer to. The other young lady walked away, and as she was telling what happened, she was also describing the lady to me. When I looked over, I saw a lady who looked just like the one she was describing to me, so I assumed that she was the one. And when she told me Satan started throwing things into my head, I was thinking, I didn't understand why she would say something about the article that was not true because I know it was of God. And that's when you know people don't have any fear of God's words. I was going to approach the young lady, and I was going to say some things that I know I should have kept in my heart because I thought she was the young lady who said it. So at my 9:00 break, I went and prayed, and before I went to break, I thought about what I was going to say when I saw her. I knew right then it was wrong because what she said was not about me, and that's what I realized it was not in God's will. And I went to pray; I asked God to forgive me and what I was thinking or about to do. He placed in my heart the prayer that I prayed that morning in his own way to let me know that she was not the one, and at that time I had peace with that young lady while I was praying. And when God gives me peace about something, that means that it is okay and there will be joy. I didn't understand why it should be joy when she tried to break my spirit, and knowing my God is supposed to be protecting me even when someone is trying to break my spirit. Later that day, a young lady came to me and told me the person who said it, gave me her name—and it was not the same lady that I assumed. Then God placed it in my spirit that I needed to go to her and ask her for my forgiveness because of what I was thinking, and for what I was about to say to her. And I truly felt bad, and it hurt me because I could have started something really bad if I had approached her the way I started to. I thank God for leading me and standing with me in that situation because that's how small things can become big. I also told her what I said and what I was thinking about. When I first saw her, she asked me where's the article in a positive way. That's why when someone gives you information, make sure that it is correct before you approach anyone. In my case, I thanked God for leading me and recognizing that it was God and not me; and after I apologized to her, there was peace in my heart again. That's when I knew I'm really being changed by God because I would never go back to someone and tell them what I was thinking. When you have God in you, it's hard to keep junk inside of you. That's why he led me to the young lady to let her know; and he continued strengthening me and encouraging me to stay in his will because it's not a pretty picture to apologize to someone when they don't even know what's going on.

Thank you, Lord, because if you are pleased with me, it makes me happy, and it makes me want to stay more in your will. PS: If it was not for you, Lord, I would not have done it. Thank you, Lord, lead me!

<<<<<<<<<<<<<<<<<<<<<<<<<<<<<<<<<<<<<<<<<<<<

Bless Your Name, Lord

All I want to do is just bless your name, Lord. I just want to bless your holy name and to praise you each and every day of my life. Lord, I just want to tell you how much I love you, Lord—body, mind, and soul. Lord, I love you for taking care of me, my family, and my friends, and anyone that is in need of your help. I just want to bless your name, Lord. Lord, I just want to thank you for your son who died for all my burdens and sins. Thank you, Lord, for loving me the way you do. Thank you, Lord, for taking me through all my storms. I just want to bless your holy name, Lord. Thank you, Lord, for showing me your way; that's why you mean so much to me, Lord. Everything that you made, Lord, in heaven and earth that I know, is so special that's why I praise your name. The joy and peace that you in stored in me, that's why it is so easy to praise you, Lord. Lord, you are everything to me—father, mother, sister, brother, teacher, lawyer, and doctor—you are all I need, Lord. I just want to bless your holy name, Lord. I just feel like thanking you right now just for your grace and mercy that follow me all my days; thank you, Lord. God, I love you, I love you; I just can't say the word that explains how I feel about you, but I know the feelings that I'm feeling right now for you is just so hard to explain. The love for you seems like the feeling is rushing through my heart and through my veins. God, what a wonderful feeling it is to be in love with you; God, right now I'm having these feelings just writing and thinking how much I love you. But, God, there's no word to explain or tell how much I love you; I'm thinking about elegant words, but no words would come to mind. But while I was thinking for a word just to describe the love that I have for my God, the Holy Spirit placed one in heart—faith. Thank you, Lord, for that word that you gave me. God, what you are saying to me, the faith that I have for you, is the same measure of love that I have for you; and the faith and love that I have for you basically means the same when you put all together. So whenever I want to express my love for you, all I have to do is say the word faith and smile because of what you're telling me, Lord. Faith is the only word I need to describe the love for you; so if there's anyone that wants to love God as much as I do, measure it in faith. So get to know this God on a personal level. And knowing what he does for you, you just can't help loving God, and you see why it's not so hard to bless and praise his holy name. I truly love you, God; thank you for allowing me to love you like you do.

<<<<<<<<<<<<<<<<<<<<<<<<<<<<<<<<<<<<<<<<<<<<

Lord, Send Down Your Holy Spirit

Lord, I'm standing here in your presence with my arms opened wide and my hands lifted up to you and with my heart opened to receive you. Lord, I need your Spirit, Lord; I need your Spirit now on my job, and in whatever words I say, Lord. I know that I'm not worthy to ask you for your Holy Spirit, but I need you, Lord. Spirit, I need you in my car, in my pathway, on the highways. Lord, please send down your Spirit right now, Lord. Dear Lord, I need your Holy Spirit to live in me so I should talk and think and treat my brothers and sisters right. Lord, bring down your Holy Spirit in my family, Lord, so they can be of your Spirit. Dear Lord, you are welcome in all our hearts because we can't do anything until you come, Lord. Thank you for living so you can share your sweet Spirit with us, Lord. We cannot do anything until you show up, Lord. God, send down your Spirit to my children, my grandchildren, my neighbors, my neighbor's children; look around us, Lord. Lord, we need you for the situation in our lives. Thank you, Holy Spirit, for every time you show up. Thank you, Lord. Lord, you know that I'm weak, that's why I need your Holy Spirit to live in me. Dear Lord, please send down your Holy Spirit in the name of Jesus; thank you, Lord!

<<<<<<<<<<<<<<<<<<<<<<<<<<<<<<<<<<<<<<<<<<<<<<

Lead Me, God

One Monday morning I went to a shop, and once I get to the parking lot and before getting out of the car, I would normally pray. While praying, I said on the end of my prayer, "God, don't let no weapon form against me prosper, and don't let no tongue be raised up against me." After I got through saying that, the Holy Spirit placed a name in my heart and called it out twice; that way, I would make sure I would not mistake the name that was called out to me. When the name came to me, I just waved my hand as if I know nothing was going to happen because of the kind of person that he is to me. But at that moment, I went back to flesh and not in God's will because right then I would have known that God was leading me because of what was going to happen. And that's why when you ask God to lead you, pay attention to every word he says to you because he knows, and he sees everything that is going to happen to you in your everyday life. In about three hours later, I asked the young man to order some tools for the job that I needed; and when I went to him to do that for me, he came up with an attitude, and he was the one I was supposed to see about ordering the parts. And when I walked away, I turned back around to let him know that the reason why I asked him to order the parts was because it wasn't in the area that we would normally order it; it was in another area. And when I did turn around to say these things to him, the Holy Spirit placed in my heart that he was talking about me, but God would not allow me to hear what he was saying. And I said to him, "You did not have to talk about me." All he did was put his head down on the desk, and at that second, he got up and walked away. I didn't understand, but I was not angry; I still had that joy and peace in my heart. And I walked away and went back to work, and we did not have anything to do with each other for the rest of the day. A young lady came to me later that day to tell me about a situation that she was in with a young lady, and she said that she was going to stop speaking to her because of the way she was treated. I told her, "Don't stop talking to her because you will lose out on your blessing, because if you do that, you will not be in God's will." I let her know what happened to me earlier that day, and I told her I caught someone talking about me. I told her that I'm not angry with the person. So if I actually heard him and I'm not angry, why should you be angry from something you heard from someone else? And when I saw him that Monday, I was still happy and full of joy and peace. I felt good and I talked to him as if nothing had happened, but it was hard for him to face me; but I continued to let him know I truly forgave him, and I was not holding anything against him, and I still felt love for him. I truly felt happy and free that I can handle a situation like that; I know I'm walking in God's will. See, if I did not walk in God's will, something small like that would have turned into something giant, and maybe both of us would have lost our jobs. That's why if you ever look at things, notice that they always start small as a seed, and they end up resulting in death, being jail, and other different kinds of situation, for something that started out small. So if you stay in God's will, when things start out small, God will stop it before it gets large. That's why God says, "Let me be in your everyday living and see what I can do for you, see if I can get in the middle of a situation before it happens." God loves us and he wants to take care of us and protect us; he doesn't want his children to be up against Satan, believe it. It wasn't him, it was Satan that he lets use him; that's why you always ask God to lead us in our everyday lives; he even let me know something was going to happen before I got out of my car by the prayer that I prayed.

Thank you, Lord, for leading me.

<<<<<<<<<<<<<<<<<<<<<<<<<<<<<<<<<<<<<<<<<<<<<<

Lead Me, Lord

Dear Lord, right now, God, I just want to thank you for all you have done for me. Thank you, Lord, thank you, Lord! I can feel you in my spirit, and it just feels so good to say that you are in my mind, body, and soul. My spirit is with you; thank you, Lord. Just to see that you can bring peace to other saints makes me feel this joy and peace in my heart. Thank you, Lord, for your Spirit to touch me like this, God. God, you are worthy to be loved and worthy to be praised. God, I love you, and right this minute I just want to tell about the experience that I have witnessed with a saint; but at this time I feel the anointing and the Holy Spirit so heavy upon me. The only words that can come out of my mouth is that I want to thank you, Lord; and I'm weeping along with those words while I'm saying it.

Christians, if you truly know how God shows up at the lowest point of your life, you would know how wonderful it is to praise him and feel his anointing upon you. And it is a good experience to praise him through the good times and also the disappointments in my life because I know at the end of the road he will be there waiting to bring me through. And thank you, Lord, because if it wasn't for those things, I would not have the faith, trust, and love that I have for you; no one can take those treasures away from me that I have inside of me. Thank you, Lord! Now let me go on with my experience with the saint! She took sick. She stated that her chest tightened up and prevented her to have problems breathing. It made her weak, and it gave her problems to stand on her own. When that happened, a young man came to me and told me what happened and asked me if I was going to pray for her. Yes, I was obedient to my Lord, and I prayed for her while I was standing there working. Yes, you can work and pray at the same time because you will be praying from your heart and not from your mouth; there are lots of jobs and schools that don't want you to pray, but saints don't let them take those rights from you because you carry God in your heart. If you are in a place and cannot pray, call it out of your heart because no one can go inside your heart and take that away from you because he will hear you and listen to you as your deepest prayer and your deepest thought comes from your heart. So, little saints, take God to school in your heart, and you'll see the difference it can make in your classroom, hallway, bathroom, and cafeteria. Because you have to take God there, so he can be active in your daily life because he loves each and every one of his children. And right after I got through praying for the saint I still was working, about five minutes after that, I decided to walk down to the room that they took her in just to see how she was doing. I did not go inside that room because I know it was forbidden to pray in that plant. As soon as I walked in, another saint asked me if I was going to pray for her, and I looked around in the room and I looked at the nurse, not knowing what she was going to say. But soon after I went into prayer with the saint, I whispered God's words in her ear, and I let her know that God loves her and that he doesn't want to see his daughter hurting. And I laid my hands on her chest to allow God to do what he needed to do through my vessel; and when I put my hands on her chest, I felt when God was releasing his power to her. I told her to receive the power that God was releasing to her and also let God breathe for her because God just wants her to cast all her cares on him.

I know God was looking down on her and was saying, "My daughter, I love you; I want to take your pain away from you; just let me have my way with you. I don't want you to go through these burdens alone; receive me in my will. I just want to give you life and more abundantly, so don't let me for such a time as now. I also would like you to keep me in your daily walk. I love you, my daughter. Let the door stay open so I can come in, so open the door to your heart and let me in. I want to bring you joy, love, and peace to your family. And I also want to carry your sickness and your needs and whatever you need me for or if you should need me to just lay your head on my arm. I love you, my daughter."

Thank you, in Jesus's name. Soon after I got through praying, the paramedics came into the room, and I walked out with no fear about losing my job because if I had to choose between my job and doing God's work, it was going to be God's work; and I know his grace and mercy would have followed me however it resulted in. Once I got to my station, I felt weak because I know that when I laid my hand on that saint, all the power of the Holy Spirit that was in me was released to the saint, and it made me weak. And I prayed and asked God to restore my strength back to me. *Thank you, Lord, for using me.*

After they took her to the hospital, the Holy Spirit let me know that she will be all right by placing the peace and joy in my heart. And when I talked to the young lady with whom I was working, I told her that the saint was going to be all right, and I asked her if she knew what I was talking about when I said that the saint will be all right. She said yes because if I said that, she knows that the Holy Spirit let me know in my spirit that she will be all right.

Thank you, God, for that saint spirit that's in you because she made it possible how everything turned out because of her faith in you. Yes, she loves you, Lord, and she also knows that you are there when she needs you; she also knows how to call upon your name, Lord. So, God, I asked you in the name of Jesus with her faith, I asked you to keep a blessing upon their home and lay the blood of Jesus upon their home. Thank you, Lord.

Visions

One Thursday night I was lying in bed, and it was placed in my heart by the Holy Spirit the voice of a spirit that sounded like my sister, and it said that my son is gone. And when she said that to me, I started saying positive words because that word *gone* sounds permanent to me, so it shook me up a little. And I knew I needed to go into prayer, and I started praying in the spirit because I didn't want Satan to go into my prayer. So when I did pray, I was praying to Jesus so he can be an intercessor and so he can direct my prayer to God. God knows he was leading me into this prayer because I know he was having me pray for someone who needed prayer, so after the prayer I went back to bed. I saw a vision of a person who was weeping; I opened and shut my eyes so the vision will disappear because at that time, I knew something was going to happen, and I knew that God was directing me to pray for someone. The next day, my sister told me about a family member who was in the hospital, and she was in a coma; and God gave me the revelation because it wasn't my son. But if he had given me a name that I could relate to, I would get up and go pray. And there was one of my family members who knew about the situation, and she was hurting and she asked me to pray and ask God for a word because of the position that she was in. The word that God gave me was that she was tired. And I know that God is going to heal her because her soul is right with God. There are all kinds of healing—soul healing, deliverance, financial healing; you can also be healed from all types of diseases. You have to have that faith. A kind of faith that is larger than a mustard seed. Yes, God wants us to start out with a mustard seed faith, but he wants our faith to grow and spread out wide and tall as trees. He wants no limitation on our faith 'cause the more faith you have, the more blessing for you. And once you get that faith and that trust in God, it will take you so high in this world just for God's glory. And the peace and joy and the soul salvation that he gives you, and the storm that you walk through, it's not yours it's God's. But he gives it to you 'cause he loves you that much it makes you feel that your are in this world, but you're not of the world because of the relationship you have with God. There can be a storm at your feet, but you are not carrying it because it's for God to carry. That's why when you go through these storms, you wonder why it doesn't affect you sometimes. Because once you give it to God, it's not yours to carry anymore. That's why you can feel so free when any storm comes to affect you; even if he calls you home, you will not be afraid because you know you will be with the Father, and if he gives you that kind of peace on earth, you know what it would be like with God in heaven.

Thank you, God, for directing my prayer, and thank you for teaching me to be obedient.

<<<<<<<<<<<<<<<<<<<<<<<<<<<<<<<<<<<<<<<<<<<<<<<<

Obedience

One Sunday I was in church, and I was sitting by a saint. I normally go into prayer during church service, but this Sunday the Holy Spirit placed in my heart to pray for the saint that was sitting next to me. I said to myself, *God, you want me to hold this saint's hand and pray for her; how am I supposed to go about doing this?* And at one point in time, I felt like I wasn't going to do it because I couldn't see myself picking up this woman's hand and start praying for her. The Holy Spirit did not tell me what to pray for; the Holy Spirit just wanted me to pray for her, so I whispered in her ear to tell her that the Holy Spirit wanted me to pray for her. And she looked toward me and smiled and gave her hand, and I went into prayer with her. After I was done, we both smiled and went back into the service. *Thank you, God, for allowing me to be obedient, and thank you for allowing me to answer your call.* See, it was not important for me to know what situation I was praying for, but it was just good to know that I was able to do God's work and, at the same time, know her obedience and her faith. I know God will bless her and keep her tied up in his blood and will give her special deliverance because she allowed me to pray for her. There was no conversation before it happened, and after church service was over, we embraced each other; and I thanked her for allowing me to be obedient to my God. And I thanked her for her obedience to God because I know God is going to truly bless her.

Thank you, God, for all the blessings that you're going to put on her and her family, in the name of Jesus. Thank you!

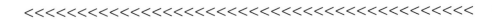

Intercession

One Friday night, our prayer group met up at the church, and we went into our usual Friday night prayer. When we got there, we went directly into prayer, and I started talking to God and asking God for forgiveness because one night I was in prayer for a saint. While I was praying, the Holy Spirit placed in my heart that she was free. With that note, I felt in my spirit that the Holy Spirit was not finished with me. I felt that he was going to show me something about that saint; and after I got through praying, I got up and I went into my room; and fear came over me. I had shut my room door, but I opened it. I would normally turn the TV off, but I turned it backed on for light because of the fear that was over me. I did not want God to show me nothing or hear anything about that saint because of my relationship with her. I was not afraid of what God was going to show me or place in my heart; I was just afraid to accept what he was going to place in my heart about that saint. But see, when you say yes to God, he will take you places that you would not want to go because of your relationship with the other saints. The Holy Spirit will also place words in your heart that you're not ready to accept the other saints.

But, God, I did say yes, and I still am saying yes, use me, Lord, use me. If there is something you have to tell me about myself or show me about myself or my loved ones, use me, Lord; there will be no fear when it comes to me doing your work, use me, Lord. When I was praying for that saint, he led me into the Psalms 23; that's how I knew there was something other than his soul being free. *Thank you, God, for trusting me.* While I was going to pray, I asked the Holy Spirit to empty everything that was inside of me, anything inside of me that would hinder my prayer. I bound myself down to the Holy Spirit; I laid everything before God. I cried out to God while I was standing and while I was putting everything outside of me that was a hindrance to him. My legs started getting weak, and where there was weakness, heaviness started removing where I was weak. My body started getting heavy, and I sat down. I started praying in the Spirit, and my body got heavier; my arms were so heavy that I could not move it. And it was as though a weight was sitting on my head. I tried to lift it up, but I couldn't; and I continued praying in the Spirit. The Holy Spirit placed in my heart that hearts will be opened, and the church will be getting a blessing. Then I continued to ask God to take me out and empty me clean, and I began transforming. I went back praying to the Spirit, and while praying in the Spirit, I knew that it was my tongue moving and suddenly the Holy Spirit took over. While I was still praying in the Spirit, the Holy Spirit placed in my heart to concentrate on the words that were coming out of my mouth, and at the same time the Holy Spirit placed in my spirit that he wanted the prayer group to come into praise and worship. But he didn't want me to tell them to come in; he wanted them to do it on their own. And while I was still praying, one of the saints who were there and was concentrating on what I was saying, stated that the Holy Spirit showed him a door with a person standing in the door, and he saw where outside of the door was clear. I also new that God directed and received my prayer to help someone with deliverance. I believed that there were more than one deliverance acts that night, and it is an awesome feeling to know that God can use me in that way. That's why I just want to stay in God's will. When I pray, I know that I get in touch with God, and I know he hears me. There can be ten thousand tongues praying against me at one time; but I have that faith to know that God will hear my voice out of the ten thousand tongues because I know what kind of relationship I have with God, and my faith is so strong. That's what God wants for all of us, just to stand with your faith, knowing God's there for you. He just wants you to have that faith so when you're sick, you can be healed, and when you're in trouble, he will be your lawyer. God says, "I am whoever you want me to be so you'll never be alone." He can be all these things and so much more to you; he loves us so much, and that's why his promise to us is that he will never leave us or forsake us even though sometimes the storms seem so much alone. But he is just a breath away; he just loves us that much. He wants us to say, "Come in, Father, I need you; you're welcome in my life, and I give myself to you and teach me your way. My door will stay open for you, Lord; just take my hand and lead me. I love you, Lord; continue teaching me to pray."

<<<<<<<<<<<<<<<<<<<<<<<<<<<<<<<<<<<<<<<<<<

Evil

One night, the Holy Spirit showed me a saint in a dream, and I was praying for him. And while I was praying for him, I placed my hand upon his chest. When I placed my hand on his chest, the Holy Spirit placed in my heart that he will not be able to help his children because his heart is filled with evil. Saint, God cannot get through your heart because you have so much in your heart that's not of God, and he wants to help you. It is sad; you'll lose out on so much especially when it comes to your children. Saint, why is there so much evil in our heart? We cannot hear from God. And yes, I know this saint that he showed me, and yes, his heart is filled with evil. When God showed me the evil in his heart, I placed my hand on his chest and I prayed. The Holy Spirit is supposed to take over, but he couldn't because all that evil was stored up in is heart and he would not let God in. And by allowing my hands to go on his heart, God was knocking to his door to come in. See, God doesn't want to give up on his children, but how could God come into a heart when it's full of evil, and you will not let God in? All God wants to say to him is, "Let me in, my son. I hear your cry, but I can't help you because you can't hear me when I speak to you. I can't lead you or direct you; what do I do or what way do I go? I know you need a lawyer, I can be that too; I know you need money, I can be that too. But let me in. I love you; take that hate out of your heart and restore it with my love. And you say you know God; God is love, not hate. How could you do my work, and how could you love your brothers or sisters? With every love you share, it's a blessing you receive. It is so easy to have love in your heart—you have joy, you have peace, and you even have deliverance. Help me, my son. I want to get into your heart, but I can't get there if you don't let me, you have to invite me into your heart. I love you, my son. Your life can also turn around. I'm not going to tell you that it doesn't always happen instantly, but it happens second by second, minute by minute, hour by hour, day by day, month by month, and year by year! I assure you that you will have peace and joy because I will be with you every step of the way; just let me walk with you. It hurts me when I can't help a child of mine. So when you cry out to God again, my son, ask for forgiveness, and I will happily forgive you because you're my son and I'm your father. And when you're happy, believe me, son, I'm happy for you too. But if you say you love me like you say, you would let me in, and you will see the flowers around you start blooming and lights will start shining. Come out of that darkness, my son; here is my hand. So now when you call my name, reach for my hand, my son, and open your heart. I love you, my son, and your children too; don't shut me out anymore, and don't let evil take over because it's never too late to open your heart to God.

Let not your heart be troubled (John 14:1).
He shall direct thy paths (Prov. 3:6).
They which be of faith are blessed (Gal. 3:9).
Your Father knoweth what things ye have need of (Matt. 6:8).

<<<<<<<<<<<<<<<<<<<<<<<<<<<<<<<<<<<<<<<<<<<<<

Miss Your Blessing

One Saturday, her mother woke her up to go to the choir rehearsal, but she really didn't want to go. She got up with an attitude even though she always attended choir rehearsals; but early that week, she asked her mother to take her to the mall to buy a couple of things that she wanted. But it was placed in her mother's heart that she was a partially good child, and she does more right than wrong, and she deserves to get the things that she wanted. The mother had already planned to take her shopping that Saturday after choir rehearsal. When she got back from the rehearsal, her mother asked her how was choir rehearsal; she walked passed her mother not saying a word, so her mother was in disbelief that she walked passed her and did not say a word. When that happened, the mother said that the trip to the mall was canceled, but we know how mothers are when it comes to their children. The mother still gave her another chance to go to the mall. Later that day, the mother's aunt and uncle came by, and she was also planning to go to the aunt's house to pray for her, not knowing if she was going to receive her or not. But look at how God turned it around. I knew he had already planned for my aunt to be prayed for because the Holy Spirit was the one that placed it in my heart to pray for her. I knew I was going over to her house again that day. See how the Holy Spirit led our walk. When they arrived at my home, we were looking at an awesome preacher on TBN with awesome words, and then she asked me to pray for her. I know God answered her prayer because she has a willing heart. And she wanted to be healed by the Holy Spirit, and she had the faith to receive it because she knows that he is an awesome God and can do all things in the name of Jesus. After the prayer, we started talking, and the little saint came up and asked for her mother to take her to the mall, and the mother told her no. She stamped her feet and mumbled some words right there, and then she truly missed her blessings that time; and she walked out of God's will being disobedient to her mother. See, saints, that's how quick you can miss your blessings if you don't stay in the will of God. God was the one that placed that in my heart to take her to the mall and to do something special for her, so if you stay in God's will all the time, you will always be blessed by the Holy Spirit. But if you move out of his will, you just don't know what's ahead for you. God puts desires in our hearts, and he directs our path. Later that day, after it happened, her mother explained to the little saint how she moved out of God's will and missed her blessing. Thank God that she realized she moved out of God's will. *God, I hope you continue to show her how easy it is to move out of your will. Thank you, Lord, for allowing her aunt to receive her blessing, and for willingly receiving your prayer and your power that flowed into her.*

That's why young people have to realize that not only when adults walk out of God's will that they will lose there blessing, but children can also walk out of God's will and lose there blessing and direction in life. So God is really showing us, and that's how we, as parents, can lose our children to Satan because Satan is just waiting on the sideline to pick them up and lead them his way. Thank you for always stepping in.

<<<<<<<<<<<<<<<<<<<<<<<<<<<<<<<<<<<<<<<<<<<<<<<<

Learning and Being Obedient

Dear God, first I want to thank you, Lord, for teaching me so I can hear from you. Thank you, Lord, for your Holy Spirit so I can talk right and my work will not go in vain. Thank you, Lord, for directing my tongue, my thoughts, my heart, my soul, and my spirit. God, I'm so happy you don't give us a spirit of fear. I had some of the experience that you had directed me, and I did not know what part I was supposed to play when things happen, such as some visions. And when you speak to my spirit and my heart, I just thought it was one of the ways you relate to me by showing me visions such as on Thursday night. The Holy Spirit placed in my heart about a person dropping her body down at the door, and at the same time, the Holy Spirit placed in my heart that nothing was wrong with her physically. After I saw the vision, I got up and prayed in the Spirit. And now I know that when God shows me a vision and speaks to my spirit, God is directing me to pray for someone even though I don't know what I'm praying for; and that's why I pray in the spirit so the Holy Spirit can be an intercessor for my prayer for whom I am praying for. I know in my spirit that God would let me know the person that I was praying for; it was just going to be a matter of time. When I went to the store the next day, there was a lady who lost her father; her nephew told her that her father had died, and she dropped to the floor crying. That's when the Holy Spirit placed in my heart that she was the person that I was praying for; so when you hear that someone out there is praying for you, believe that because the Holy Spirit do lead intercessors to pray for his loved ones. That's why God wants to teach all his children to open their hearts, to receive their teaching from God because nothing just happens; God knows what's going to happen, when it's going to happen, what time it's going to happen, and how long it's going to take for his glory to be revealed. That's why I want to be like God; and to be like God, who is the better teacher to teach you about God's ways than God himself. So when God teaches you and when God taught me, it was nothing that happened overnight. It seems like it happens in series, and there are lots of tests that you have to take for the Holy Spirit to go to the next level. I heard once upon a time that being a child of God is easy if you don't want the wisdom, patience, experience, compassion, understanding, and love that God teaches you to have. It was back in the 1980s when I was working in the steel plant. I met a Caucasian man who was a racist, and he was also the plant manager. I was also the local union vice president. This man and I always had contact with each other. He would always appear negative when it comes to certain employees, and he was not a caring person. One day, he was in the plant looking for me, and when he found me, he asked me to pray for him. When I heard him with disbelief—not on my face, but also in my head—I couldn't believe that he would actually ask me, who is of a different culture, to pray for him, knowing the way he was. And not only that, I wondered how he knows me as a praying person because I didn't know myself in that way, but I knew I had a compassionate heart. And when someone tells me about their problems or their sickness, it seems as if I'm the one having the problem or sickness at that time, not knowing I was really carrying their burden until God releases it. I thought that I was just praying, and I left it at that; and when he asked me to pray, I told him yes, I would gladly pray for him. And I went into prayer for him, and after I talked to God for him about his condition in a compassionate way like I was the one with cancer and like I was in pain, I left it at that; and I forgot that I even prayed for him. I did not even thank God, and I did not even ask in Jesus's name, not knowing that I was in training and God was teaching me how to pray, and I actually forgot that I prayed for him until one day, he came to me, thanking me for praying for him because he was now cancer free. At that time, I can't remember what I said to him, but I know that I did not give God his glory. But God knows that when I pray to him, it was truly from my heart, and I prayed in truth; and at the same time, God knows that I was in training—to be taught how to pray from the Holy Spirit. When God leads you to pray and the Holy Spirit is using you, it doesn't matter what kind of spirit that particular person had, he was still God's child. And when he asked for that prayer, he must have known God and know that he could receive healing from God. Now God is taking me back to let me know I gave you the compassion and heart that you will be able to pray for all my children in spite of their ways because God is love, and when he places that love in your heart, you can return his love back to your sisters and brothers. And that's why it was so easy for me to pray and talk to God about his condition.

Thank you, Lord, for using me for such a time like that. Thank you, Lord!

There was another Caucasian young man who was working with me, and he was also in poor health. And when he told me everything that was wrong with him, it stuck in my heart. And it was a burden in the bottom of my stomach, not knowing that was his burden I was carrying. And I went in pray for him, and I will never forget about it. I would see him walking around the plant, and you can tell he was in pain because his facial color had changed, and it hurt me to see him like that. And the burden came back, and then I would go back and pray again, not knowing that God was listening to me. And at the same time, God was leading me into prayer. All the sickness that this man was telling me about, you would think that God was calling him home. After a couple years later, his health started improving; it was amazing how his health seemed so perfect again, not knowing that God actually heard the praise that went out for him. One time, I thought he was just claiming sickness and nothing was wrong with him, but there was a lot going on with him. I really knew that he was sick, not knowing that God healed him. This man is now living a normal life with his wife and his children. *Thanks, God, for healing him, and thanks, God, for leading me to pray for him. Thanks, God, for the burden you placed in my stomach to pray for him, and thanks, God, for the compassionate heart. Thanks, God, I don't choose who to pray for; and, God, I thank you for placing these events that happen in the past to bring it back in the present to let me know that you lead me to pray for those two people.* I didn't know anything about praying and healing; and as a matter of a fact, I didn't believe that God healed.

Thank you, God, for placing that anointing on me that I didn't know I had. I knew that I always felt like I was out of place, and I always felt that I couldn't fit in. Even when I am with friends, I felt like I was the oddball, and now I see why, God, because you always had your hand on me. And if I could go back to those days where I felt so all alone, God, I would do it all over again just know that I would do it for your glory because at the same time you still gave me a special feeling because at the same time I still couldn't describe what was going on, but I still had joy. Now I know you, Lord, and I'm saying yes to you, Lord; so continue using me in your will. Thank you, Lord.

While I was working at the steel plant, the plant manager offered me a position for a foreman job; and when he offered it to me, I told him, "Yes, I would take it if I can be Angie." He replied, "That's the reason I'm offering it to you, because I want you to stay, Angie." And with that note, I would treat everyone the way I wanted to be treated, and it doesn't matter who the person is. I would treat them with respect, not knowing that that's the right way and that it is also walking in God's will. When I was offered this position, there were so many people hating me because I was offered a position and I took it, and they did not understand that the president of the plant offered it to me; but he was inspired by God. When you have all these men working with you and they hate you for that, you know God was right there to give me his strength, and he will never leave me or forsake me. I prayed every chance that I had because it was not easy not knowing that God had put me there to see if I could stand that position because he had a position for me in his army. So if I could stand all those negatives that were thrown at me, I will still stand. I know it was God, and I know he was going to take me through the storm. I told a few men who are working at the plant that there were a lot of people angry with me, but they were angry at the wrong person. And the person they should be mad with is God because God was the one who placed it in the president's heart, and he didn't even know that he was inspired by God to give me that position. But at that time, I knew it was God, and it was just a young man that worked with men. I would always have large jobs, and I would have to assign these jobs to the workers. It was this particular man, and he wanted the position that was given to me. He hated me for it, and to be honest, he was qualified for that job; but see what God can do when he wants you to have a job at a workplace, and he was a great worker. And I know I was going to need him to assist me with these large tasks that I had, so I know I needed to pray and ask God to change his heart. I prayed and I prayed. One day I came home, and I just went on my knees, and I asked God, "Why are you taking so long? I need you to work on his heart because he was so evil to me." I know he was going to change his heart, but I felt like I needed it to happen right away, not knowing you need to be patient, be of good courage, and learn how to wait on God, and learn how to stand still, and while standing, stay in God's will. I didn't know about standing and peace be still, just to wait on God; all I know is that there was a God I could go to when I need help in any situation. And I continued talking to God, and I started feeling that peace, and I started laughing and talking to God, not knowing that you can have conversations like that with God, not knowing that he will still listen to you in that way. Right then and there, I knew I was getting closer to God and was beginning a relationship. It was a week later that the man's heart had changed. His hate for me moved out of is heart, and we actually worked as a team in the maintenance department. God was changing hearts in a positive way. I thank God because when I was going through that, no one in my family knew what I was going through because I took my problems to God as I knew he was going to handle it. I knew how to go to God, and I knew God taught me how to pray for the changes in the hearts. God put me in those situations to be strong and to get to know what he can do for us if we just depend and trust in him. He will definitely show us that the way is God's way, and if you are walking in God's way, you would know how to treat people. And the love and joy he stores in your heart, you would definitely give it back because you have to love and care for people in order to truly pray for one another. When you pray for someone, it goes so deep in your heart, and it is so deep in your soul. When it is real, you can feel what the other person feels; that's when you know you are doing God's work. Yes, God is truly alive; use me, Lord, use me. Six months later, the president of the plant offered me another position, and it was the maintenance assistant superintendent. Yes, God planted that seed in the president's heart because at that period, they did not want women in the maintenance department, so you know that it was suicide having a woman as head of the maintenance department. There were about sixty men working in the maintenance department, and it was hard for them to accept me as the head of the department. There was a man with that position, but there were many complaints on how he was treating the employees. So it's just like I was placed there to make a difference. The president knew I would be treating everyone equally, and I thank God for his favor as my supervisors did not like women being in that plant because that was a plant just for men. It was devastating for him to know that I was the supervisor of the department. I knew his dislike for me, just for being a woman; but after I got the job, their hearts changed toward me in a good way. And I knew it had to have been God because they treated me with love, respect, and kindness. And to know these people—and if anyone didn't know what was going on—I honestly knew that it was God's favor the way they accepted me because that's the only way they would have. Thank God for his strength because that's the only way one could have walked his walk when you personally know you're not accepted, and you could walk that walk with strength and you could make it. No one knew how much I stayed on my knees praying during that time because I knew I needed God to carry me through, but he will always give you someone that you could call on. *Thank you, God, for that because you knew I needed it.* This is how God shows me that I truly have compassion for someone. One day we were in a meeting, and we were talking about the jobs that needed to be done; the employee that I replaced was in the meeting also. The assignment was needed to be done in my department, so the question was directed to me though it would have been directed to him. I think that's when he truly realized that I was his supervisor, and I saw the hurt on his face. It was devastating, and it really hurt me to see him like that. I couldn't stand, nor did I want to see him like that again. After the meeting, I went to the engineer's office, and I told him I wanted to speak with him. I let him know the experience that happened and how much that man was hurt; and it looked like it did something to him, just to know he did not want to work in a position lower than mine. I asked him when we're in any morning meetings, "If there are any assignments, direct your assignment to him and not to me." That way, he wouldn't get his spirit broken. And when I told him that, he just looked at me with a surpised look on his face as if it was unbelievable for me to say those words to him. At the time I did not realize I was doing God's work, not knowing I was in training because if I can give up a position for a man's spirit not to be broken, I would. Imagine what I can do for God, to give God his glory, because it's not about Angie, it's about God. It's not about my feelings of my title, it's about God. I did not understand then, but I did know that I did a good thing. And yes, I would do it again because if I can help mend a heart for God, I would. Now I understand why I can never carry hate in my heart for someone if they do me wrong. He has broken my spirit many times. Thank God, when he slapped me on my right cheek. I gave him my left cheek.

And I did that only for you, Lord, that's why I want to surrender every part of my body to you, dwell in your present, and base in your Spirit, and give you permission to move in my heart just for you, Lord. God, thank you for your experience; it even helps me to know myself. Thank you for taking me back there, God, that's wisdom, experience, and hope because if you don't have wisdom and hope, you cannot walk in truth doing God's work, and you have to truly, truly love God. He's first and last in your life, tied up in Jesus's blood, and his words stand the negative that comes up against you, and all you can say is it doesn't matter because I know who I am. Thank you, Lord, for staying in my life.

One Tuesday, I was on my way from work, and while I was driving, I was in praise and worship. The Holy Spirit placed in my heart a young man's name so I could talk to him. When I got home late that evening, I tried to contact him, but I could not find him till the next day. When I saw him, I did not say anything, and I looked at him again. I knew I had to call him so that I can be obedient to God. I needed to talk to him, not knowing what I was going to say; and he came over. I let him know that the Holy Spirit placed in my heart to speak to him. I informed him that there is something that he is going to do or get himself into a situation that he can't get himself out of, and that's why the Holy Spirit wanted me to talk and pray with him. At the time I was talking to him, I could tell that he was hurting; and the question I was asking him, I knew by his spirit there was some truth in it. When I told him that the Holy Spirit wanted me to talk to him, he held his head down, and I knew he knew exactly what I was saying that's why he could not look me in my eye when I was speaking, as though I knew something. I let him know then and there that I did not know anything because the Holy Spirit did not tell me anything; he just wanted me to speak with him. See, God knows and loves his children, and when they are hurting, God will send someone to them if they just stand and listen and open their hearts. They will listen at that time, and they want help at that time. But when they get away from you and they get back out, there they're lost again. Yes, I'm hurting because whenever Satan puts his hands on our children, it hurts when you know God wants to help, and Satan wants to keep them out there. Satan just cheers them on and promotes trouble that they get into.

God, give me the wisdom that I need to reach our children; give me the knowledge and understanding that I can bring them to you. Lord, you gave me this compassionate heart; now let me do what I need to do for you for your glory. God, there are too many children out there, lost; some of them had bad things done to them while they were growing up.

Someone broke their spirits, and no one was there to teach them how to forgive. But if they only knew that if someone does evil to you, forgive them, and if you don't, that person has power over your happiness, joy, and peace. You will begin to hate, and you will also do things to get back at others just because of things that happened to you. Little brothers and little sisters, if you need help on how to help forgive and you cannot forgive on your own, trust God and ask God to help you to forgive, and ask God to take that darkness off your life so you can walk in that light of joy. Believe me, after you stop hating and begin receiving God's love along with patience, you will feel light as if you're flying and is full of joy, and you just want to do whatever there is to please God; and that's walking in God's will and not walking in no man's jail. God wants us to be free and not lock down with any stronghold tying us down.

God, I would like to thank you, in the name of Jesus, for all the prayer warriors and all the intercessors that will be praying for all the saints. Thank you, Lord, I love you!

One night I had this dream that I wanted to build a small one-room house so I could spend time with the Lord. So there was a man whom I asked to build a house for me, and he agreed to build this house, and we were deciding how to place the house. I decided that I wanted the house to sit by the trees and lots of tall grass. After he disappeared, I knew there was something else I wanted this man to put in this house; and I was looking for him, not knowing what I was going to tell him, but I still knew that there was something else that I felt I needed to put in this house. Yes, it sounds strange, but God puts desires in your heart and you don't even know what it is. That's why I love God so much. I decided to walk in my house, and when I opened the door, I saw a man sitting down. He was not the same man who agreed to build my house for the Lord, but at the time, I felt like I knew him. I was happy to see him, and at the same time, I could not believe he was sitting in my house; but I still didn't know who he was. When I saw the pictures that he was drawing, I shouted out to him, "How did you know that's what I want to put in my house?"

Those were pictures of the biblical days of God, and also, some were holy pictures. The pictures were going to be carved on the wall because they were going to be permanent pictures; and the man said to me that he was going to add two more rooms to this house and that he will also put it directly behind my house. He said that it will not be in the field. The more I thought about this dream the Holy Spirit placed in my heart, the more it appeared the man was Nathan the prophet. That's how that man knew exactly what was in my heart, and I did not even know because he was a messenger from God. *Thank you, Lord, for sending Nathan to my house.* I knew there was something special about this dream, so I asked a saint about it. She was telling me about Solomon building a house for the Lord because he loves God just that much, and she told me to go to First Kings 3:5-6. Solomon wanted wisdom and understanding and didn't ask anything for himself; and while I was reading it, I said to myself, "Those are all the things that I always ask God for." But I did not say that to the saint because I felt that she would think I was just saying that.

Thank you, Lord, for granting my prayer when I asked you for your wisdom and understanding and even patience along with it. I asked you these things in peace and just to know you are really paying attention to me; it's an awesome feeling, God. It makes me love you more and makes me want to do your work more because all I care about is to make you happy. I truly want to stay in your will, and everything I do is for your glory. I will not be able to do it without your wisdom, your understanding, or your sweet spirit upon me. Thank You, God, for storing these treasures upon me and for continuing to let me grow. God, thank you for letting me know that you know my heart even though I know that you know it is a blessing to me for you to call on someone as powerful as Nathan and Solomon to let me know my deepest thoughts in my heart. All I want is to understand your words so that I can give back to your saints. God, you were shown to me in the book of First Kings, chapter 3. Yes, God, your words showed me at once before you told me that you knew the hearts of the godly and ungodly; and thanks, God, that you know my heart, so that places me with the godly. I am so appreciative that you chose me to be one of your servers. God, that's why my love for you gets even stronger today than yesterday, and that makes me want to serve you even more. It is so awesome for you to take the time out to show me that you know the inner thoughts of my heart.

Once I was explaining to other saints my relationship with God and how God is using me in unbelievable events, because they don't know my inner heart and they don't really believe that God is still healing hearts, healing souls, healing diseases, and that he has the power to use anyone that is open to him. It's not about me, but it's about what I would like to do for God and his glory.

Thank you, Lord, for the love that you have for me, and thank you for the promise that you gave to us; you will never leave or forsake us. And, God, my promise to you is I will never leave you or forsake you.

One day I called this minister because I was feeling low, and I needed someone spiritual to talk to. There was some spiritual things that I was going through, so when I called this minister I was telling her some of the events, and I was trying to explain to her that God was truly using me because I wanted her to believe me. I thought she would have given me some spiritual input, so I said to her that God is truly using me, and she replied back to me with a spiritual let down. "God uses everyone in a way," she said. I knew she was not the person I needed to talk to for spiritual advice, but I said to her that God does not use everyone because everyone won't let God in their hearts to be used by God. You have to make sure you want to work for God, surrender your heart, and give up all the old and pick up the new garment and have the ability to stand whenever darts come at you. Once your heart is open, you have a special relationship with God, and he will speak to you in so many different ways that you would know, and no one else would understand you. You may sound or look weird, but you can't be ashamed to do what God wants you to do. Just to stand on his word because there are people in high position at church who will come to you and say things to break your spirit, but they don't even realize that Satan is using them too. That's why I said God does not use everyone because everyone does not want to be ready to make that stand because it can be lonely sometimes. But you just have to remember that God will be right there to give you the strength you need because God just don't want some of us; he truly wants all his children to be ready the day Jesus comes back. There was a saint whom I work with, and we were talking about how things are going on in the churches and that God spoke to me and told me that out every hundred only 20 percent of the people know him; and he said he will reveal those that are not of God. He was responding to me as though what I was saying was not true, and I continued standing on the words that God gave me because I told him that God gave those words to me, and I'm going to stand on those words. He continued denying that God spoke to me in this way. The conversation had to stop because the break was over, so we went back to work. He told me before we departed that we can finish the conversation after work. Later, the Holy Spirit placed in my heart that when God gives me words and I tell someone about it and the person doesn't believe, I don't have to prove anything to anyone. God's words will stand when no other words stand; so when God gives you a word, it does not matter if the person has a high position in the church and if they tell you that they don't believe the word came from God. Just stand, and I mean stand on what you know when God is speaking to you. The more I stand on God's words, the taller I get. The taller I become, the closer I get to God. And you will not fall because you are standing upon a rock, and the rock is God. So stay faithful and stay strong and hold on to your beliefs when it comes to God because he will surely take you through all storms and conquer your giant; and your giant is anything you're facing that you can't handle. Just invite Jesus and turn it over to him. Once you give it to Jesus, don't take it back, and you will see how free you will feel. Jesus carries your burden and takes it off you so you can be free. Even though you know the burden is there, it's still on the outside, and Jesus is working it out for you. But your faith would have to be there along with your surrendering. Thank you, Jesus, for just bearing the cross for our sins. Thank you, Lord, in Jesus's name! Yes, I surrender my all to you, Lord.

<<<<<<<<<<<<<<<<<<<<<<<<<<<<<<<<<<<<<<<<<<<<<

Last Word in Obedience

Thank you, Lord, for making one of your saints obedient to your word. There was a minister who said that the Holy Spirit told him to move out from the church that he was ministering at. And some of the congregation did not understand why he came back the way he did, but they just don't understand when the Holy Spirit told him to stop; that wasn't the last word. There was some misunderstanding going on in the church that is not of God, and sometimes God will move saints to get other matters straightened out. And one day when I was in prayer, I was asking God with all the mixing up in that church, "Why did you not speak to me in my spirit or speak to my heart to tell me whether I should stay or leave?" I was saying other words to him because I know that God would not put me in a place with ungodly acts going on because of the kind of person that I am. By God being silent to me, I knew he wanted me to stand, and so I did stand. One day I met with the minister, and what he was saying to me was some of the same words that I was crying out to God. He said that God was also giving him scriptures to let him know that it was time to go back to the church, or less damnation will fall on him. See, saints, that was the Holy Spirit's last words in that situation. God would have you take a walk that no one understands, no one but you and the Holy Spirit and true believers; and if anyone was involved in this situation, all God wanted them to do is stand and pray, and he would show you what was truly going on. When you pray, don't pray with your lips; let your prayer come from the central part of your heart, and God will truly show you the way. And when this minister came back, he said he was in God's glory, so that also gave him time spent with God and to get him to a place that he will stay in God's will, because that's what God wanted for him—to get high in his glory so he can use him the way God wants to without interference from other saints. That's why the Holy Spirit did place in my heart that he wanted to use this minister, but he had to let some people go. I did not understand when he said let some people go; I would had never known that they would have been leaving the church. I would never have thought the people who left were the ones the Holy Spirit was talking about. When the Holy Spirit had placed the words in my heart that he would have to let some people free so God can use him, I thought the Holy Spirit meant for them not to spend as much time with the minister, but to see that was Ann's way of thinking and not God's. The minister came back to the church, and then the church was separated; some people stayed and there were some people left. But nothing just happens; God can see, God can hear, God knows our thoughts even when we don't know it. He also knew that everything happened in this situation was going to happen. God was showing and telling dreams, visions, and giving his words in our hearts. He was giving warnings, but no one was listening or understanding the words that were coming out, or their ears were not opened for the words. God thanks you for your obedience in having your heart opened and for hearing his words. Even though he didn't want to leave, he still did because of his obedience. Sometimes we do not understand when God is using someone. When they move out on faith, we call them crazy—why did that person do that? he should not have done it, he was wrong to do it that way, he was wrong to come the way he did. Please, saint, *stop*. Please, saint, get to know the God you are praying to; you're praising his name, but God wants you to get to know his ways, get to know his voice, and to understand him when he says stop. You don't have to know what he means right there and then, but *stop*. God doesn't give you reasons to do whatever he wants you to do; he will tell you the beginning now, and he will give you the end later. That's why you have to have a relationship with God so you will know his ways. He would never leave you or forsake you; that is his promise to all of us.

One night, God showed me in a dream why one of the saints left the church. We were in a room, and there were three of us there. He said that he will tell me why he left the church, and he began whispering in my ear. And it seemed that I didn't hear anything; but he whispered, so I walked closer and put my ears to his lips. All I heard was a saint's name and rumors, and I could not hear anything else. I was trying my best to hear what he was saying, but maybe I was not supposed to hear all of it right now. When he was talking, I was responding with three different sentences, telling him why he should stay; and I can't remember the words that I was saying to him. But I kept telling him he should stand because he will be the leader of that congregation one day. If he had just stood through the storm while everything was going wrong.

Stand, my son, let me be your strength were you are weak. I love you, and I promise that I will not forsake you. Look at all the joy that I have given you, and I have much more for you. Just show me that you can stand for my glory. Yes, you could be the leader of this church one day if you had stood, but I still love you in spite of the decision you've made because you're my son, and I will always love you. I just wanted to see if you were going to stand; that's all we have to do to bring God in our situation through praise, and that's the word that the Holy Spirit will always place in my heart when any situation starts occurring. God will always say, "Pray." And it's always good to know that you need to stand. God will not lead you into the wilderness without his blessings. If you want to separate yourself from someone or someplace, make sure it is what God wants and not man because that can happen if you're not in the will of God. Through the storm and while the wind is blowing, there are weak branches that fall from the tree. That will give you word of advice that are not of God. So when the wind comes against you, just say peace be still, and it will soon disappear. Just give it some time with patience, and God will definitely guide you through the storm. Sometimes the road seems dark and long, but if you stay in God's will, you will be given peace through the storm. Just have faith, trust in God, and humble yourself to him.

Thank you, Lord, because nothing just happens with the situation that caused the separation in that church.

The Holy Spirit placed me in the presence of eight members of the church. I was led to tell them what the Holy Spirit placed in my heart. First, it was that the minister had to let some people go. God can use him highly, and all saints will be revealed—those who are of God and those who are not of God. There are only 20 percent out of every one hundred who know God and who know other things that were being said. He also wants me to tell them that I am a prophet called by the Holy Spirit and to also inform the people that I did not meet face-to-face. And he also let them know that the Holy Spirit led me to talk to them, not knowing why until the Holy Spirit gave me the revelation and the confirmation of the situation that was going on in the church. God did not want what happened to happen. He wanted them to know that he was sending a messenger to them. They were listening, but they just didn't hear me. Maybe their ears were closed because I told them that I am a prophet, and I can understand that there are false prophets out there. But believe me, I am not one. I did not ask for this job, but I will be obedient to God. I will say what he wants me to say, and I will go where he wants me to go because I know it's helping someone who wants to hear the word that truly comes from God. And when I told God, "Yes, I will take this job," I meant this from the deepest and most secret place in my heart. And when he sent me to the minister of the church, I knew that he was skeptical about me when I told him that I am a prophet. But God had to take us on a road to show him who I truly was, but you don't know how to receive a prophet because God will bless you when you receive one of his faithful servants. Yes, I can say it with boldness now. Yes, I am one of his faithful servants, and I will let no one discourage me from holding on to my trust, my faith, and the love that I have for God. No one will send me to the wrong path because my beliefs are in God. Yes, it can happen if I move out of God's will, and that's easy to happen. But when you are truly touched intimately by the Holy Spirit, and that power that he has on you when you walk, you know you walk in God's strength because it seems like you're walking in the air. It seems like your problem is so light, and you just want to embrace someone and share it so you can enjoy the peace and the love that God has in store for you. It's so easy to refuse, but just open your heart. *God, I cast all my cares to you, I want none of them for myself, just come on in my heart, take control of my life, walk with me every minute of the day. My problem is your problem, my sickness is your sickness, and my trouble is your trouble. God, thank you for letting me cast my cares on you.*

One day I was in prayer, and the Holy Spirit called this saint by name and said that the reason why this person left was because this saint was not anchored in God. That's why the Holy Spirit placed me in this saint's presence, and that's why he was not listening to what I was saying and what God was placing in my heart. He knew what I was saying, but he was not ready to receive the words from me, not knowing he was truly talking to a prophet. This saint is not anchored in God because those words that God gave me are enough to put fear in a person if they are of God, because God doesn't want any of his saints to walk out of his will because God loves us; he wants to give us all the source that we need. He doesn't want any of us to be out there in the wilderness; that's the kind of God we serve. He loves us, and he doesn't want anyone to break anyone's spirit. Even though one is not anchored in the Holy Spirit, God still has his hands open waiting for anyone.

Thank you, Lord, for providing the covenant that you have over us.

One day a saint and I were in a conversation about what was going on in the church and about what her decision was going to be. When we were done talking, I went into prayer, and the Holy Spirit placed in my heart that all she needed to do is to go and pray and the Holy Spirit will tell her what she needed to know. See, just stand and talk to God when any situation happens. Stop, stand, and pray until God gives you an answer. God will give you an answer through your prayer and faith, and trust him enough to know that he will guide you in the right path and direction. You have to be obedient to God when he gives you your answer because it's for God's glory and for your blessings. That's why it's always good to stay prayed up because you don't know what situation you will be facing. That's why the Holy Bible tells us to keep the armor of God. And when you do, keep it on that means, and always stay in the word of pray, and every time Satan comes against you, you have your armor of protection on—God's word. Saints, whatever storm you are facing, to pray is your first occupation. God promises never to leave or forsake us.

Thank you, Lord, for God's not being an author of confusion. God and confusion cannot stay in the same house; God wants his house to be a place of prayer because God is the prince of peace. Thank you, Lord.

<<<<<<<<<<<<<<<<<<<<<<<<<<<<<<<<<<<<<<<<<<

Stand

Any situation may occur in our life. It may just be a test for our faith to stand for the glory of God. When the mountain seems so tall and you see no ending, don't take that situation and run. It may be a time when God is giving us a chance to start trusting in him. See, when I run, I don't run in faith. I try to run out of the situation that is going on, and I run right out of God's will. Satan will attack me in all negative ways, and that's when I realize that it's about me and not God; and that's when I will know that I will face more trials and more mountains in my path. God only wants us to have the patience and the faith, so the Holy Spirit wants to teach me his way. He wants "to trust me, depend on me, call my name, talk to me, and pray to me. I will give you the advice that you need. I will guide you and lead you. I will tell you when to talk and not to talk. I can see what's ahead of your life; just give me a chance. I will help you with minor as well as large situations. My child, learn how to stand in a storm. I will walk you through it, hand in hand, if you let me. I will walk with you every day. I will go to bed at night with you, and I will get up in the morning when you do. I will have a brace around you; but if you stop for a second, you will feel my love around you. See,

I will never leave you; just recognize that I'm just that close to you. Please stand and move that burden away from your heart, so you can hear me, so if you focus on the Holy Spirit and not yourself, you will understand when I tell you joy comes in the morning. See, I'm hurt when you walk away from me. I love you. Please learn how to stand so you can get to know my voice. You can feel when I'm in your presence and my love, that I will store in your heart the power that I have. I can be whoever you want me to be and also do whatever you want me to do, just ask in the name of Jesus. The gifts that I have to store in your heart, see with the trust and faith you have in me, and I can heal in so many ways. I can heal a broken heart. I can heal if you have burden in your heart. I can heal diseases. I can heal souls. And I can even heal finance. See you have a God with all kinds of powers. He can even heal situations in your home. Yes, my Holy Spirit can come down with a bundle of love if you just allow him to come down in your heart. I will come down in a glorious way. It will feel like your body was transformed to someone else's body. The love, peace, joy; the lightness on your feet I move the weight of hate, the jealousy, the anger, and I will give you a forgiving heart. No, you cannot love me with hate, so you have to allow me to store love in your heart because love is God. I just want to be in your everyday walk. You don't have to have no reasons to let the mountains and trials get you down because that's my job to take you through, and that's my promise to you to. I love you, child. I see your today, your yesterday, and your tomorrow. Those are my plans. See, nothing just happens, but all you have to do is weather the storm, and I'll be right there by your side. Sometimes it feels so hard, and I know it's hard, my child, but if you just remember to pray and stay in my will, your tomorrow will be fulfilled with gladness. That's my promise to you. That's why I want you to stand and surrender yourself to me, and I will teach you how to solve the situations in your life with a gift of wisdom and an understanding heart and much more gifts that I have for you. Just humble yourself and turn your heart my way, and God's way is the best way. You will never go wrong."

Lord, all I want is to stretch my holy hands to you in one accord with my brothers and sisters. We know you are the source of our lives, and the strength of our lives, and the light of our salvation. You will be moving mountains in our live, and the trials that you will be taking us through. Lord, we praise your holy name. We praise you, Lord, so that you can work out things that are going to happen tomorrow, next week, next month, and the next year.

That's why my praise and worship is so important to me because nothing just happens. God knows our future. The Holy Spirit also loves a praiser and worshipper. It's so awesome to be in God's presence. That's my hobby, and the only hobby I ever have is to serve God. I remember on job applications and various applications they will always ask, "What is your hobby?" I will never answer because it never seemed like there was not anything that's interesting. One day I went to get some new glasses, and on the order form, it asked various questions. And to my surprise, it asked me what was my hobby. For the first time I could have answered it by saying, "I love to be a servant of the Holy Spirit because there was nothing I love to do more than serving God."

<<<<<<<<<<<<<<<<<<<<<<<<<<<<<<<<<<<<<<<<<<<

Phone

One day I loaned a friend my cell phone because his job was farther than mine. And one day the Holy Spirit showed me a vision that he had the phone in his shirt pocket, and it showed me that the phone fell out of his pocket. I started to call him, but I did not because at that time it did not seem important because it was a cell phone, and I wasn't thinking what it would cost me to get another. I would have called him and told him to take it out of his pocket, but I did not call him. A week later, I called him for my phone, and he brought the phone to my house. When he came in, he sat on the chair, and I looked at him. And it looked as if he was putting his thoughts together. And a few seconds later, he pulled the phone out, and the phone was separated into two pieces. He started coming up with some stories, and I really didn't want to take it to heart because of what the Holy Spirit had already shown me. Yes, I was angry at myself because I didn't do anything about it; but I couldn't be angry with him, so I listened for a couple of minutes. I just told him, "Please don't say nothing else," because he was making up excuses of what happened to the phone. When he said he had it in his shirt pocket and it fell out, I told him I already knew what happened, and deep down I felt like I was responsible because I did not call him. But to replace that phone cost nearly $200, and it wasn't that I didn't trust or believe the Holy Spirit, it was that I didn't think that the phone was important enough for me to respond to the Holy Spirit. But now if the Holy Spirit shows me a vision as little as my shoes being untied, I will respond quickly.

Thank you, God, just for being in my life. I love you so much. I can find no words to describe how much I love you, but the word of faith because that's the word you put in my heart. I love you, God, just because you are God.

<<<<<<<<<<<<<<<<<<<<<<<<<<<<<<<<<<<<<<<<<<<<<

What the Love of God Means to Me

What love of God means to me is to have a compassionate heart for your neighbors. Love is to have the joy in your heart for neighbors. Love is not to enjoy rumors about your neighbors while their spirit is being broken. Love is not jealously. Love is when your neighbor is being blessed with everything they need, and you just help them enjoy their happiness. Love is for me to love you, and you to love me. If you have love stored in you, well, you know you love God because God is love, and you will be able to see the spiritual gift that God stored in you. The love of God in me will bless you, and the love of God in me will heal your brokenness. The love of God in me will heal your finances. See, because the love of God is truly stored in me, and because of the love of God, I can love you because of the love that God stored in me. It makes it so easy to love you and give it back. That's why God is everything to me. Your are my life and breath of fresh air, and to me, that's why I bow before the king—and that king is my Jesus—because of the love I have in me. The love that I have in me that gives me peace when things happen in my life. It seems not fair because the love that I have in me that is of God gives me the peace to stand even when he doesn't speak to my spirit or to my heart. I still know I will stand because of the love I have in me. I know God will guide me and lead me in the direction that I need to go because of the love and trust I have in God.

Thank you, God, for letting the Holy Spirit transfer my mind and more of my heart, and for teaching me how to love.

Yes, it's an awesome feeling, and it's hard to explain when you meet someone for the first time and you say I love you, but it is really not my love that I'm sharing—it's the love of God that is in me. That's why it is so easy to pray for my neighbors and feel their burden because the love of God that is in me.

Thank you, Lord, for your sweet Holy Spirit that dwells within my heart. God, please keep me and steer me in your will so I will not lose this love of peace that I have in me. Continue using me, Lord, because all I want to do is to continue giving you the highest praise of hallelujah. When I feel the sweet joy run through my body, God, it is so good to know you, and it is so good to have this kind of relationship with you. Thank you for teaching me your way. Thank you for teaching me how to stand in a storm. Thank you, Lord, for letting me love others even when I know they are taking about me, I can still love them. Even if they hurt me in ways that it can turn into hate, but I can still love them. But I know that in order for me to love you I still have to love them in spite of. Thank you, God, for allowing me to be able to walk in your strength when I'm weak until I can pick my strength back on my own so I can love back again.

You will get weak in this walk with God because you will always have Satan trying to attack you in so many ways so you'll lose the love that you have for God. See, when you say you are of God and you know you are of God, you can stand to your neighbor and say in authority that if you know the same God, you know me. If I know God, I should know you. If you know God, you should know me. If we cannot identify each other's spirit, then one of us is not of God, and it's not me because I know who I am, and I'm of God because I know God is in me. So be able to stand for your sisters and brothers in Christ if you know God, and believe it or not, the Holy Spirit will award you for your obedience. So when you stand up for them, you stand for God.

One day I was at one of my former jobs, and at that job, they had a table that we would have to be at every morning and afternoon. One afternoon, our team was in the team room. And as usual, we were sitting down, and a lot of talks were going on, and two young men were talking to each other. While they were talking, they were using profanity. One of the young men was using it more than the other, and I looked at him and shook my head, and I said a word to him. His response was, "What's wrong, miss?" He kept talking as if it was okay for us to listen to the words that he was saying. The next day I mentioned to the young man that this other young man was using profanity in the team room. I asked him to talk to him, but let it be one-on-one because I didn't want anything to happen to him, but at the same time I didn't feel as though I had to listen to those words that are not of God. When you are walking to follow the Holy Spirit, and you want the Holy Spirit within you, those words really disturb the inside of you and that was one of my reasons why I said something about it; it grieved my spirit. When I told the young man to talk to him one-on-one, he stated that he would call a meeting to talk to a few of the young men to ask them if they used profanity in the room. They all said no. They also said they didn't hear anyone use it either. They still wanted to let them know that when in the team room, no one uses profanity. When they all came out of the meeting, they were angry because I said something about it. That's not all, I don't feel that I should be the subject to it, so they all talked about me and tried to break my spirit and called me all kinds of words except a child of God. So you know that left me by myself standing with God. That Monday morning, a young man came and approached me and said someone told him that I accused him of cursing in the team room. When he did approach me, he was just kidding around. At the same time, it was loud, and I didn't feel as though I should have been approached that way. He also accused me of putting this man's job on the line. I told him that it didn't start out that way because nothing was going to happen to him. If I thought that something would have happened, I probably would not have said anything. He said that I couldn't change that man if he wanted to use profanity. I told him that I was not trying to change him; I was not going to just sit there and listen to him. He asked me why didn't I talk to the young man, and he also stated that if I was a Christian, I should be able to talk to anyone. He said his minister preaches that if you know God and you actually read his book, anyone that speaks that kind of language, God gives you the okay to walk in a different direction. He continued, "Just read the book of Proverbs, and that's why I respect you and everyone else, and I stay my distance because I know who I am about. If they want to use that kind of language, I was not going to stay in their way or stay in their company so they won't feel uncomfortable." At the same time, this young man whom I was talking to had never disrespected me as we spoke; things just got out of hand when he came over to talk that morning. After we got through talking, I was not angry with him, but it just seemed that I couldn't stay in that spot; I had to get away. I don't know where I was going or what I was going to say, but I know I needed to move from that spot. I was walking down the hall, and I ended up going to the bathroom, and I went in to pray. After the prayer, I still wasn't angry, but while I was talking to God, I know I wasn't telling God about this young man because when someone does something to me, I go to God and let him know someone has hurt me, and I ask him what he is going to do. Instead, I just prayed and talked to God, because I wasn't angry; but God placed in my heart: "You don'thave to say a word, I would handle John John for you.", And when that was placed in my heart, I felt a little fear because

I didn't wanted anything bad to happen because, believe it or not, God knew this was going to happen that's why he led me to pray for him two weeks before it happened. So now at this time, it seems as if everyone hated me and talked about me as though I was a part of Satan's war, but thank God, I knew the truth to stand on. I thought it was over with, until two weeks later I received a phone call to meet in the office at ten o'clock that morning. I didn't know what was going on, but I knew I had put in for a job. I thought they were calling me for an interview, but at the same time, I was wondering why they wanted me in the office. This gentlemen called me in the office, and that's when I really thought it was an interview, but when I sat down and heard his response to me, he was telling me about the incident that happened. He asked me how I felt about the young man approaching me the way he did, and if he was one of the young men who were using profanity that's why he approached me. He asked me if I heard someone using profanity. I said yes, and I let him know that everyone whom they interviewed said that they did not hear anyone using profanity. But he replied that if I said I heard someone using profanity, I was telling the truth. He asked me what would I like done to this young man. I told him that this young man had never disrespected me, and I assured him that he will never approach me in the manner that he did because we spoke to each other, but not in words. God showed me in his spirit that if he had to do that again, it would never happen that way; that's what God showed me in his spirit. The gentlemen whom I was talking to told me that someone called the 800 number and told them about the situation that happened. When some people heard that, they thought it was wrong for that person to call; but see, God placed it in that person's heart to call the 800 number so I wouldn't be the one to say something about what happened to anyone. That's what the Holy Spirit meant when he said I wouldn't have to say a word, he will handle John John for me. At the same time, God was testing me to see how I was going to respond to that also, and see if I was going to take the opportunity to hurt him, but instead, I did what the Holy Spirit would have done. And that's when I said I don't want to see nothing happen to him. *Thank you, God, for giving me that compassionate heart.* After that day, it became worst because no one new what was going on as everyone was throwing darts, and everyone had one side of the story, and nothing but negative words were being tossed around. I just stood alone with God. One morning in my usual praise and worship, I felt like I had enough, and I prayed and I talked to God. I told my God that I didn't do anything wrong so now "you give me your strength to take this walk in this building because my strength is not strong enough to endure all the darts that was thrown at me so, God, now you move in me. You lift my head up." When I walk into that building, I felt light, I had joy, and I had peace. And I felt like if anyone had said anything to me, they couldn't break my spirit anymore because I was walking with God and the ones that didn't see me I wanted them to just look at me. I might be alone with flesh, but I know I have it all with God. After that day, it didn't matter if they spoke, it didn't matter if they turned their heads when they saw me, it just didn't matter because I had my God with me. When I had enough of loneliness, I had to remember where is my strength, who is my strength, where is my joy; and who gives me my joy but God, and I'm not going to let any man take that away from me.

Lord, I love you, and no one will ever take my joy. God, if you can feed a multitude with two loaves of bread and five fish, with our faith what can you do for us? Jesus, you are the best thing that ever happened to me.

Yes, God wants us to know that we depend on everything he does for us, and it gives God joy to know that we trust and depend on him just that much. That's why when I'm at work or in church or in my car, it just doesn't matter where I'm at, if I can't talk to God aloud, I talk to him under my breath because I know the Holy Spirit can hear me, and he also will answer me. God will also lead me and guide me because that's the kind of prayer I will ask him for. Yes, God will answer our prayer as long as we invite God in our everyday step. God is not an all-weather God; he's the kind of God that will stand with you in any storm that comes your way. He just wants you to say, "God, I need you and I need you now because you promise not to leave me or forsake me. Now as little as a glass of water, Lord, I need you." And he will place in someone's heart to call you or stop by just to give you that glass of water. All you have to do is ask him and trust in him. And he will do the impossible just because of your faith; that's why he's such an awesome God.

"Trust me, my children, open you heart to me and surrender yourself to me; give your body as a living sacrifice. Trust me enough to do that with your faith; your strength and my strength, we can move mountains that even try to get in your way because that's what I would do for my children. I love you all."

Thank you, God, for being such an awesome father to us. I love you and I will always love you even more than yesterday. I just love you.

The reason why I don't like any kind of words spoken into my spirit is because I have the Holy Spirit living in me. That's why I should be able to choose the words planted in my spirit—words that are of God and not words that are not of God—because the word of God stirs up the Holy Spirit that is in you. That's all I want in me, just to get closer to God.

God, you say let everything that have breath praise the Lord and also give you the honor and glory. God, thank you for the air that I breathe and the Holy Spirit that is in me. God, I just want to thank you for those gifts, and thank you because I can't live without it. God, that is why I would do anything that is asked of me. God, I need you, and I am desperate for your presence because if it was not for the air that I breathe, I would not be here living right now. Just thinking about the air that I'm inhaling, the one you gave to Adam and Eve, if we had to pay for this air that you have given to us in this cycle world, we probably would not be able to afford the air. Thank you, God, for breathing your air into us. God, you also said that who should ever thirst for your righteousness should be filled. Just stand by me, Lord, and direct my path. I just love your Holy Spirit living in me. God, it is truly a blessing to just to be in your presence. God, draw me near to your cross so I can continue to stay in your will. Thank you, Lord, for continuing directing my path!

<<<<<<<<<<<<<<<<<<<<<<<<<<<<<<<<<<<<<<<<<<<<<

The Cross

One day I was in praise and worship, and while I was worshiping, I was in the presence of God. The presence was so heavy it was just as if I was in a thick cloud. I had both arms stretched out wide, and it seems like I was standing tall. All a sudden, it seems as if I was face-to-face with Jesus on the cross. I did not see his face clearly, but I saw it just enough to know that that was Jesus's face. My arm felt like someone was holding it up, but at the same time it was stretched out on a cross, and there was no weight or anything that I was feeling like I was holding it myself. The presence was so awesome because I felt his presence so close to me. For a second, he started moving away from me, and his face drew away from me in a light moving swiftly, and I was standing, trying to follow that light. I could feel the movement in my leg; I felt the veins were tightening up, feeling as if they were struggling, but I couldn't move my feet. It seemed like I lost my focus in worship, and I came out, and the vision was over. It was an awesome feeling being that close to Jesus because the power felt so heavy like thick clouds. *Thank you, Jesus, for that experience.* That's why when I go into praise and worship, I bow myself to the Holy Spirit and move everything out of me that is not of God so I can be in the presence of the Lord. I love the joy that he stored in me; it seems as if it gives me newness in my body. Thank you, Lord.

One day I was working at this company with a young lady, and one day she told me that her back was hurting. I didn't say anything about her back when she was talking about it. We started another conversation, so that next week she said that her back was not hurting her; maybe it was her coming back to work, and she had to get used to the work again because she was out from work for about six months or more. She also told me that she had a bone disease, so when it gets cold, her back hurts. So the next day while we were working, I saw when she was holding her back. It gave me the same feeling in my body, so I knew her back was still hurting her. I didn't say anything; I just looked at her. The next couple days I prayed for her back, and when I went back to work a couple days later, I planned to ask her if she believed in healing from God, and she said yes. I told her that I had prayed for her, and she asked me what did I pray about. I told her that I saw that her back was still hurting her, and I prayed for God to touch her back because she needed to work, and she can't work in that condition. When I told her that, she replied with a bright smile that that's probably why her back suddenly stopped hurting and she did not know why. It stopped hurting her. And that particular day, it was cold, and her back was still not hurting her. I asked her if she thanked God for removing the pain, and at that time, she started thanking God. She said that she knew God had blessed her a lot, but she had never taken the time out to thank God for the blessings that God gave her. From this day on, she said she will start praying more to God, and she will start thanking God more for the blessing he puts upon her life.

Thank you, God, for touching my life in such an awesome way. Thank you, God, for listening to my prayer for someone else. Thank you, God, for being such an awesome God, and thank you, God, for being a caring God. Thank you, God, for just being you!

One night I had a dream that my daughter was doing things out of God's will. I was concerned about her, and I was following her around. It even felt bad when she moved out. I moved in a room next to her just to keep my eyes on her because I didn't want any harm to come against her. She would always listen to me, but at the same time, she would always do her own thing, and she didn't care what she was doing as long as she was happy; and that was the scary part. At the same time, I still felt the presence of the Lord in the mix of it all, and when I woke up, I started praying, and I asked God not to let Satan attack her mind, and not to let Satan take a stronghold of her. I asked God to plead the blood over her body and tie her in a knot and tangle her up in the blood of his precious

son, Jesus. Later that day, God gave me a revelation. Parents, when you are a friend of God, your children can go anywhere; they can be in any danger, and God wants us to know he will always have his eyes on them. Wherever they go, he will be right there with them. Whatever they do, he will have his arms around them. Whatever trouble they get into, he will hide them. Parents, just keep your eyes on the sparrow; it's not for you, it's for your children. Do it for your children so they can have that covering of the Holy Spirit because that was not me following her nor being in the next bed. The Holy Spirit just wanted us to know that's how he does when our children moves away from him. So you, as parents, continue to do my work, I will cover my children.
     Thank you, Lord.

One day my daughter and I were in a conversation with a young man, and I was telling her that his aunt was saying some things about him that were not of God and told my daughter about some of the things she told me. I didn't want him in her life if that's what he was doing. At that time, that was just a talk of a mother's love, and she replies to me, did the Holy Spirit tell me something about him? Believe me, I really wanted to say yes, but I told her that no, I did not ask God anything about him. She surprised me when she asked me that, and it made me happy to know that she knows that God is real. And at the same time, God is using me in that way. I would never say the Holy Spirit tells me something when he did not, and the way she trusted me to tell her the trust, I have that kind of trust in God too. If God gives me a word, I will say that he gave me a word, and if God did not give me a word, I would say that too because you can work yourself out of God's anointing, and damnation will fall on me. So I will not go around to say that God gave me a word, spoke to my heart, showed me visions, and gave me dreams. Believe me, I will fall quicker and harder than a person who does things, which are not of God just to pretend that I'm doing things for my glory and not for God's. With God's glory, you will always stand, and with your glory, you will fall.

So, God, continue bringing down your Holy Spirit on me. Bind me with your Holy Spirit so I can continue staying in your will and know how to talk and work through your wisdom. Thank you, Lord, for my daughter to believe in you, trust in you; and I hope one day I can say she is in love with you as much as I am or more. When her day comes, she will have the joy that no one can break her spirit when they come against her. Thank you, God because you promised me that she will be saved, and I know you will cover her until that day comes. Thank you for blessing me with her.

Dear God, I want to lock my eyes on Jesus. I want to walk in the Spirit so I can be fruitful and not flesh full. I know, if I are not focused on God, I will not be able to get the gentleness that I need to be a servant of God. And also, I will not be able to help a broken spirit or anyone that needs a word from God. Thank you, God, for allowing me to be your righteous servant. God, I ask you to continue staying in every step that I make so I can do the right things for you and your glory.

One day I was asked if I go to parties, and I replied to the saint no. I don't want to listen to different cycles of music. She told me that nothing is wrong with listening to that type of music, and I told her that when you are working for God, you have to stay in words that are positive and in the word of God. Yes, I don't see anything wrong with that if that's what you want, but for myself, I would rather stay prayed up in full armor, so when the Holy Spirit sends to me someone to pray for or to give a word to, I will always have my full armor on. And that means I will always stay in God's word and stay prayed up. That way I would not receive negative seeds because I want to be about my father's business and not about mine.

Thank you, God, for showing me when my children are on a high mountain and on the edge about to fall. God, you will give them a word to pull them back in, and your mountain can be drugs, alcohol, and any type of abuse. Thank you, God, for hearing my prayer. Thank you, God, for leading me to stay in your will, and thank you, Lord, for seeking your face. Thank you, God, for the covenant that you have over my family and also over other saints. God, I love living in your world, and when your rain of love falls down on me, it gives a fantastic feeling; and I just want to go praise and worship more. God, your peace, your joy, and your happiness that you stored in me right along with your Holy Spirit, I would like to thank you for. I'm still seeking after your heart, so when I'm weak you can give me strength, so I can do the right things for your glory, so I would not live my days in vain. Thank you, Lord, for trusting me.

One day a saint was telling me that he had a flat tire, and he changed his tire. The tire that he replaced weren't good tires. He said he would not be able to buy tires for his truck until he gets paid again; so by that note, this is telling me I needed to go and pray for him every night, day, and hour. When I pray, I would involve him in it and ask God to cover the tires on his truck. One morning, I saw his truck on the way going to work, and God led me in a prayer. While I was near his truck, I put my right hand up toward his truck, and I started to pray in the Spirit to ask God to take care of his tires and to shield him from any danger. While I was praying, it seemed as if my car was moving, but I was not going anywhere until I was finished praying. After I got through praying, I went on to work. Later that day, I saw the saint, and he was telling me about the experience he had that day with his tires. He said he was hearing a loud tapping noise, and he thought it was his tires about to bust again. He turned his radio off so he could continue to monitor the noise that he was hearing. He kept on driving, and every time he stopped at one of his stores, he would thank Jesus for getting him there safe. He drove about sixty miles going store to store, and every time he got to a store, he would continue to say thank you to Jesus. After he got off from work, he had a friend to follow him home because he was going to pick up his father-in-law's truck, and he wanted his friend to drop him off. While his friend was riding behind him, his friend noticed how his tire was shaking, and how it looked like it was going to come off. Once he got to his house, his friend got out of his car and asked him if he was sure his tire was not loose; and when they checked it, it was loose. I thanked God for leading me to pray that morning, and I thanked God that he was inviting God with him every step of the way. And he did not realize that that was what he was doing. When he was telling me that, all I did was listen; I did not even tell him that I was praying for him that morning. God is an awesome God, and you will see what he will do for you if you invite him in our daily life. That's all God wants us to know. Just call on Jesus's name, and he will be there for you; just call him saint, and he will hear you because that's the love he has for you.

<<<<<<<<<<<<<<<<<<<<<<<<<<<<<<<<<<<<<<<<<<<

How God Leads You in a Prayer

One day I saw this saint and she was telling me about her friend's son, and she was telling me that he was in a car accident and it left him paralyzed. He was placed in a nursing home because of their financial situation, and his mother would just go and see him every day. She was not able to go and see him for about a week, and while she was absent from the nursing home, her son got sick. The saints who were working there did not realize the young man had feelings because the condition that he was in was because they neglect taking good care of him, which caused his sickness, and he ended up in the hospital in intensive care. When his mother went to see him, his mother saw how he was hurting inside by seeing tears rolling down his face, and when she told me that, the Holy Spirit just stirred up inside of me. She was telling me this so I could pray for them later that day, but the Holy Spirit would not allow me to wait that long; he sent me into prayer right then and there. The Holy Spirit came down so powerfully on us when we went into prayer. I kept praying in the Spirit, and she also felt the power of the Holy Spirit. After we got through praying, the Holy Spirit told me that it is going to be a breakthrough for them. And after I told her that, she told me that was awesome for the

Holy Spirit to give me that word because they sent a prayer cloth to a breakthrough ministry, and they were waiting for that breakthrough. After that, we both thanked God and walked away, and when I saw her later that day, she told me that she had called her friend and told her about the experience that we had. And while she was talking to her, she felt the Holy Spirit right then and there, and she received the word that was given to her. She also got a breakthrough that day when she spoke to the nurse, and the nurse told her everything that happened to her son. So right then and there, we knew that the Holy Spirit touched her heart so she could tell the mother the truth about her son's sickness. I thanked God for me being obedient and for keeping me stay prayed up so he can use me.

Thank you, God, for the training you have given me. There will be many more blessings for that family because they invited God into their life, and she has a praying friend.

One night, God showed me in a dream that there was a lady I was talking to about a situation that was going on in her church, and I was telling her that all she has to do is stay in God's will. And to stay in God's will, she will be doing the right thing; and every time she would say something, I kept saying that she stay in God's will. While I was talking to her, there was another saint bringing another saint into the church and *trying* to steal money from the church. While I was talking to the saint about staying in God's will, there was a saint listening to me, and all of a sudden her negative ways turned into positive. There were also two ministers listening to what I was saying, and they agreed and were also happy to hear the conversation. One of the ministers called me to come to the pulpit. When he called me, I only walked halfway to the pulpit, and I was standing by the saint whose ways quickly changed in accordance with God's will. So the minister came down to both of us, and he was telling us to clap our hands together. The saint has a ball in her hand that she was trying to break open. She couldn't break it open because it was sealed tight, so the minister came down and broke it open with a hammer. It

was opened, and it was full of anointing water. He anointed my
head with a cross, and he also anointed the saint who was standing
next to me with a cross too.

One day, the Holy Spirit placed in my heart that he wanted me
to stay as I am. When he told me this, I just *assumed* he was talking
about the way he wanted me to dress because I and another saint
were talking about how a prophet was saying; she only wore white.
So I thought the Holy Spirit wanted me to stay as I am. While
writing this book, he gave me the revelation that he was speaking
about my heart, not the way I dressed. God doesn't care about
the way you dress; he is only concerned about your heart. In your
heart, he only wants you to be compassionate, loving, humble,
understanding, trusting, and faithful, and to be able to stand up
for his word in any situation that comes up, knowing that God is
God if you have to stand alone.

Dear God, this is my prayer to you. I'm asking you, in the name of
Jesus. I am your servant, and I'm asking for an understanding heart to
judge thy people that I may discern between good and bad. Thank you,
Lord. God, once you told me that you inspired me to write books 1 and
2 because of the love that I have for you. When you placed it in my spirit,
I said yes. I thank you for choosing me to be the author.

But as the author, I don't have anything to say about myself,
and I don't want to say anything about myself because it's not
about me, it's about being obedient to the Holy Spirit, and it's
not for me to take away God's glory. Though I can say one thing
about myself, and that's that I am a child of God. None of these
events would have occurred if the Holy Spirit hadn't given me
dreams, visions, spoken to my heart and spirit. It was such a good
experience for me to be chosen to be a part of this project, and
to see how God works in action. God has gifts for all of us if we'll
just be obedient to his callings, and if we don't, he will just pass it
to someone else. So when you say yes to God, say yes from your
heart, mind, and soul. If it doesn't come from your heart, God
will find another obedient heart to carry out his task.

So thank you, Lord, for using me in such a way that you did. And now, God, I must continue standing so that you can lead me in the direction that you want me to go, and I will be patient in my stand because of the love that I have for you. God, I know you don't put desires in our hearts to open the door for you to come in, but, God, I'm asking you to put desires into my heart so that I can keep the door to my heart unlocked and opened so you can come in freely and direct me in any way you want me to go. I'm asking you, God, in the name of Jesus, please don't ever take your anointing away from me because I don't want to live without your presence because that is something devastating to loose from you, God. So, God, continue to mold my heart and transform my mind to your will. When I bow in praise and worship before you, Lord, I'm asking you to keep my family under your blood, in your blood. I'm asking you, in the name of Jesus, to direct their hearts to you, God. Thank you, Lord, because I know it will be done. God, I need your love in my home. I need you to fill your love in every small crack or hole that is in my home; seal it with your love. God, if your love is in our home, I know God is in our home and there will be deliverance, healing; chain won't be broken, and Satan will flee. God, we know you are love, and if we allow it, love can break anything that is evil. That's why, God, we know you want us to stand.

Let God move into your heart, and it will start with God's love. It will free you from that heavy dark cloud that carries the weight in your heart. God cannot work in a heart that has hate, envy, jealousy, and too much pride to let God use you. Stop and stand. God wants us to stand like an ocean, like when the wave is at peace. That's when you can see the beauty of the ocean. When we stand, God wants us to show the beauty that's in ourselves, and that's when God knows that he can work in our hearts because he can lead us and guide us into our gifts with anointing. When a hard wave comes back upon our lives and it turns it to be a storm, we can say peace be still in faith knowing it will be done because that starts our walk with God and the beginning of being anchored upon that rock that is God. Our Lord has a love for us that no evil work can separate us from the love that is within God's heart that he holds for us. God wants our love to come from our heart, not our lips. When you tell God, "Yes, I will do what you want me to do in Jesus's name," God knows which is real, the lips or the heart. When you surrender your heart to God and he says come as you are, you can go to God with a broken spirit. Any bad habit, finance, broken marriage, lost loved ones, God is standing with arms opened, waiting for those words so that he can carry your storm for you. He said to me once, "I will work in the hearts." When you let God work in your heart, he will carry all your pain in a way that you don't even realize that you are in a storm. So once you give your life or body to God as a sacrifice to him, you will be set free. Yes, you will have storms coming your way, but if you let God in, it will become easier to walk through for his glory. So if you know it is God's glory, then it will be victory for you; and grace and mercy will follow you.

Thank you, Lord, for your grace; thank you, Lord for you mercy; thank you, Lord, for your faithfulness; and thank you, Lord, for your love that will endurance in us forever.

One night my daughter came to me and asked me where was my manuscript because she wanted to give to my daughter-in-law so that she could revise it. I told her where it could be found so that she could give it to her. The next day my daughter-in-law called me and asked me if my daughter told me what happened with the pages that were recently typed. I told her no, and she told me what happened with the pages. When she told me what happened, I don't know what feelings I had but it felt as if nothing happened. So when she asked my daughter if I had anger, my daughter said yes, but she just assumed because she knew that I didn't have any backup information to retype my manuscript. At that time, I didn't have any anger in my heart, but I don't know why I didn't have any anger but peace was still in my heart. When she came over so that we could restore the information that was lost at that time, I still felt as if nothing had happened. I just felt as if I would have to send what was left of the manuscript. So while typing, some things did come back to mind. While she was typing, I wanted to ask her if she did pray, and ask God to send the information back to me, but instead, I prayed. Later, I did ask her if she prayed, and she said that yes she did ask God to bring the information back. I thanked God that she knows who to go to in times when a situation is not going right, and she may not know that while she was praying, God was probably working in my heart to receive what she told me the way she did. At the same time, I feel like God was testing me to see what I am about, if I am of God or am I a so-called Christian. See, so-called Christians will act in a way "it's about me", or say some thing to break someone's spirit. I could have also said something that could destroy the relationship we had with our family because of just one small word that was evil. See, that's how so-called Christians act, but instead, I did what Jesus would have done. I stood patiently and did not say a word, and God replaced everything that was lost back in my heart. See, if I did not act the way Jesus would have done, and I sat and thought it was about me and not God and did not keep peace in our family, God would have known that my heart was not pure with him when I said it's not about me, it's about God. Now I see that I am more a true worker for God than ever because I depended on God to restore everything back to me. I thanked my daughter-in-law for trusting me enough to come to me the way she did and also to know that God is involved in this family. I thanked God for that, and I asked God, in the name of Jesus, to continue to bless her family and household because she put God first in the situation when it happened. That's all God asks of us—to trust in him in any situation whether it is large or small. I asked her how I responded to her, and she said I did not appear to be upset about the situation. See, that's what God means when he says, "Stay in my will, I will lead you. I will let you know what to say and when to say it, and how long it will take you before you can say it."

Thank you, God, for guiding my tongue. God, guide my tongue in a way that if anything should come out, let it be of you. If it's for me not to say, bury it in my heart, my mind, and my soul. I thank you, God, and I thank you for blessing me with my daughter-in-law.

<<<<<<<<<<<<<<<<<<<<<<<<<<<<<<<<<<<<<<<<<<<<

The Question That I Was Asked

A saint called me one evening, and she said that she had a question to ask me. When she was saying that to me, I was praying within, asking Jesus to move in me so that he could answer the question for me. The first question she asked me was if I do believe that God is real. The first word that came to me was *air*, the air that God gives us to breathe. She seemed as though she wanted to hear something else. I replied that the air that God gives us to breathe gives us life, and God made the earth. If it wasn't God to you, then it would have to be a higher power that did these things. Maybe there had to be a higher power to have made the moon, sun, light, and darkness; but I know God is my higher power, and he is real to me. The life that he gave we couldn't do anything else without the air that he gives us to breathe. So nothing else comes to mind but the gifts that God gave me to start my journey with him—life. So yes, I believe that God is real and much alive to me. Maybe to you there's another higher power, but to me God is my higher power. The second question she asked was, how do I know it's God's voice when he speaks to me? I replied that I know God's voice by my relationship with God. I have a day-by-day communication with God. When he speaks to my heart, I listen until I get to recognize his voice, and I give him all my attention. If you have someone in your life that you love body, mind, and soul, and you want to please that person, you would recognize everything about that person. Not only that, if you know any friends and family, and you communicate with them on a daily business, then you would recognize their voice. If they called you from their home, state, or from out of town, and you are not face-to-face with whom you're talking to, wouldn't you recognize that person's voice, and would you be able to call that person by name? Anyone that comes after that, you would know their voices even if it's fifty saints calling you. And if you have a relationship and communication with them, you will know the difference in their voice. If there's someone that calls you for the first time or or if there is someone that you seldom speak with, you probably would question who you were speaking with. That's why God wants to have this special relationship with us so that when he comes to us, we will be able to recognize God's voice, his presence, and his love that he pours into our hearts. *Thank you, God, for allowing me to get to know you in that way.* The third question she asked was if I do believe what is stated in the Bible. My reply was that if you know God and you study the books in the Bible with an open mind, you will know that the Bible is teaching the truth. In the Bible there are teachers, prophets, believers, nonbelievers, and evangelists just like we have today. I also told her about Abraham and Moses and other saints in the Bible who have sinned; they repented by going back to God and seeking his heart and forgiveness. That's what is being done today in this society. We commit adultery, take lives, steal, healing, deliverance, and wars. All these events are happening today and also happened in the Bible. Some of us repent and ask for forgiveness from God, and he will restore the anointing that he gave to us. God will use us again because we seek after his heart. When you seek after God's heart, you have to have love for him. When God opened the Red Sea to free the people from the pharaoh, we can relate in this society by seeing how he is freeing us from our financial problems, freeing us from diseases, and freeing us from all sins. Those things are pharaohs in this society. The fourth question she asked was, how do I know when God is telling me something about her? I replied that whenever someone comes to me about a situation—and when I say situation, I mean a number of different things—I told her I would always go into prayer. And I will pray about a situation that I was told about, and I would wait for the Holy Spirit to place a dream, visions, or speak to my heart and my spirit. Sometimes he will have me prophesize while we are speaking to one another. Sometimes while we are speaking, he will give me a word. In order for God to give me a word, I would have to stay prayed up. When I say prayed up, I mean that I have to constantly stay in prayer and stay in conversation with God.

When someone comes to me and I don't pray, God would give me a word because I always stay in communication with him. At that time, I didn't know that I must stay in communication with God for him to use me in such a way that he is using me. Even when he used me through healing, I have to stay prayed up and faithful, and the person who's being prayed for would have to have just as much faith to receive the healing from God. Even though the Holy Spirit told me all I have to do is lay hands and he would do the healing, I still would have to have faith to know that God is using me to heal the person. There are times that God would give me a word about someone that he would not allow me to speak about, and he would also give me dreams, visions, and words that would not come to pass until two or three years later, but it would still come to pass. Sometimes he would give me a word but not allow me to say anything until the right setting because that person may not be ready to hear from me what God has to say. That's when God works on the heart to let that person know that that word is from God. I also let her know that God will not send me to someone who is not ready to receive his word. Sometimes saints may play you off at first, but they will eventually let you know that the word the Holy Spirit gave you lines up with the situation that is going on with their lives. I know that God would not lie about the situations he placed in my heart because I trust God, and I have faith in God because I know that everything he shows me is the truth; and that's what gives me the strength to stand for God. There are saints that don't believe that God is real, but God actually has vessels for him to use, and I am one of his willing vessels. So whenever God gives me a word for someone, I will go where God wants me to go and say what God wants me to say because I know he won't send me alone, and I know that he is with me. That makes it easier for me to do his work because God's word says that he will never leave you nor forsake you. Being one of God's special child, I know that he would never leave me nor forsake me especially while doing his work willingly. When she asked me once to ask God what she should do in a situation, God replied to me, "Home, home." At that time before I could answer her, she said, "I think I'm coming home." And the Holy Spirit placed it in my heart home, home; and it was four of us on the phone talking and praying so I know God placed those words in my spirit for her. Since I was already prayed up, it seemed as though it was half a second, and God gave me those words for her. See, God knows when you need an answer right away, and he knows when you need to wait on a word. However, you get his word; it's for his glory because it will come to pass. God loved each and every one of us, and when we ask anything in the name of Jesus, he will answer and he will give you positive words to help. The situation may not be positive, but he will give you a word that will come out in a positive way. God doesn't want our burdens to be a hindrance for us to get to know him. If we keep burdens in our hearts, then it will not be opened to give us a chance to know God. To know God is to love God not because of all the things he would do for your family, your friends, and even your enemies. You just have to love God because of who he is, not what he can do for you, but what he can do for others. It's an awesome feeling when he can use me in such a way to help him.

So, God, use me. I just love to be one of your righteous servants. When she asked me those questions, God, I don't know if she was asking for herself, or if she was asking to give me something to think about because some of those answers I don't think I would have answered the way I did if it wasn't the way I felt for you. God, this made me realize day to day how important it is to have you in my life, and even by asking those questions, I realized how much I really know you. When I say I know you, I feel in my spirit how much I love you. The love that I have for you, God, sometimes when I think about you, it brings tears to come out of my eyes without crying. It is so excellent, God, just to be in your presence. God, I want to be a loyal friend to you, not an all-weather friend that I have dealt with. Thank you, God, for teaching me how a loyal friend should be. Thank you for walking hand in hand in my life with me. Thank you for teaching me your ways. Thank you for increasing more of the Holy Spirit in me and not flesh. God, I know I need more work on my spirit, so I'm asking you, in the name of Jesus, to clean my heart, wash my heart, and go deep in the bottom so that you can pull out what's not of God in me. So I can be more faithful and loyal because I know what a loyal friend should be like. That's what I want to be to you, not only a daughter, but a loyal friend. If I have to stand alone to witness your name, I will because I know that you will be right there with me because you are a loyal friend to me. Thank you for the strength that I had during this walk with you. When negative came against me, I was able to stand because I knew you were there with me. When they speak negative about this book, I know that it is about you and not me. But, God, I ask you to forgive them because they do not know that they are speaking about you. God, I ask you to bless them and keep your watchful eyes on their families. Thank you, Lord, for the joy and peace. Thank you for teaching me how to forgive so that I can keep this joy that you stored in my heart. Thank you for the faithfulness that I have for you.

<<<<<<<<<<<<<<<<<<<<<<<<<<<<<<<<<<<<<<<<<<<<

My Inner Man

God, we ask you in the name of Jesus. We ask you, Lord, please help us to control our weakness of temptations, of patience; our weakness by guiding our mouths; our weakness of our attitude, jealousy, hate; our weakness of making wrong choices; our weakness against speaking negative toward other saints; our weakness against drinking alcoholic beverage; our weakness against committing adultery; and our weakness of anger. Thank you, Lord, for letting us look into a mirror and show us the reflection that we don't want to be. Thank you, Lord, for showing us that we cannot love you with all these sins inside us. So, God, we ask you in the name of Jesus give us the strength that we need to remove everything that is in us that is not of you and the spirits that we did not call out that is in ourselves. Go as far in us as you can to pull any evilness that we have inside ourselves so when we go to look back in the mirror again, we can see a picture of you, and we can be free to use the gift that you stored in us. And the only spirit that we should carry in us is the spirit of your love, God. Thank you, Jesus!

<<<<<<<<<<<<<<<<<<<<<<<<<<<<<<<<<<<<<<<<<<<<<<<<

Grace and Mercy

One day my daughter went to a convenient store alone, and while she was at the store, a gentleman approached her and asked her if he can take a picture of her. After he took a picture, he wanted to ask questions to put in the newspaper. She responded no and kept on walking, and when she told me about it, it was two weeks later. I told her I was happy that she did not stay and continue carrying on a conversation with him because during that time, there were men trying to lower young people in cars, and I was glad to know that she was obedient to my word that she should not be having any conversations with strangers. The next day it stayed on my mind, and I asked her if she believed the young man, and she replied yes, but she still kept on walking. I told her that the young man could have seen that she was not an adult; she was still a child. And if he would have taken a picture of her, he would need a parent's consent. I told her what could have happened if she responded to the young man if he was not telling her the truth. I asked her if she remembered the dream that the Holy Spirit showed me that he will always be here with her wherever she goes, and I feel like that was a time that the Holy Spirit was there to focus her mind and to keep walking and not paying attention what the man was all about. Yes, God says he will be there to take us through any trials and tribulations if we seek his heart, and his grace and mercy will follow us and guide us through a situation that you don't even know you are walking in.

God, thank you for your grace and mercy, for following her. And I will seek you, God, for the rest of my life just knowing your presence is surrounding us. God, I thank you for stepping in whenever the situation wants to attach us. God, teach me even more how to live my way in my home so I can teach my family your way. God, tell me your likes and your dislikes, and once that seed is planted in me I will truly know how to treat my brothers and sisters because I want your grace and mercy to follow my family the rest of their lives. God, you say, "I am who you want me to be," and, God, you showed us in this situation that you are an awesome protector. Thank you, Lord, for being there in our time of need.

<<<<<<<<<<<<<<<<<<<<<<<<<<<<<<<<<<<<<<<<<<<<

Someone Is Praying for Me, Someone Is Praying for Me

When someone says they are praying for you, you should believe it in faith because God has placed saints on earth to be an intercessor so they can be righteous whenever they go into prayer. One night I was in prayer in bed, and as I was praying and talking to Jesus, I heard a voice say "momma" twice. I would normally have fear in my heart whenever I hear voices or see visions. Or I would try to place what's going on or what voices I hear, though it's not for me to know whom I'm praying for. I just need to be obedient and do what God has chosen me to do. And that's to go and pray. So when I first heard the male's voice, it ran on my mind that it could be my son, but the voice was not familiar. The voice was calm, but you know that it was crying out for help. I then went into prayer, knowing that's what God wanted me to do for his saint. There was one day in my hometown where I met this young lady that I knew. Her daughter was accused of committing a serious crime, and when I heard of the situation that happened, the Holy Spirit laid a burden on me so that I could go into prayer for her. I went into the third day, and I prayed to God that Sunday morning. I asked God what he wanted me to do because I was still carrying the burden. I asked him if he was going to give me a word, or to send me somewhere, or even show me a vision because I was still feeling the burden that he laid upon me. It was right there that he placed in my heart that the mother was not able to pray so he wanted me to continue to pray. Later that day when I was praying, the Holy Spirit placed in my heart why I was carrying the burden in the bottom of my stomach, and I could feel the pain so clearly because the Holy Spirit said the reason why I was carrying the burden in my stomach, instead of my heart, was because I would not have been able to pray or cry out to God or get a word from God because my heart would have been filled. There is no way I would have received a message from God if my heart was full. That's when you say cast your burden on the Lord and leave your heart open so you can pray, praise him, worship him, and he will give you a word or lead you or guide you in the direction that he wants you to go. Also, his word says, "I will never leave nor forsake you." He will always send someone who is righteous and knows how to send a righteous prayer, and that person will have to have faith to know that God will answer your prayer. When one of God's saints should have a broken spirit or a heavy pain in the heart, God will have someone to be there for them. If you believe and know this God will bring you through, he will bring you through your troubles because that's how much God loves us. So never feel that you are alone because God is always watching over us, and he knows when we need someone to intercede a prayer for us. You may not know that someone is praying, but believe me, God has someone in place for such a time when you need a prayer.

Thank you, Lord, for you grace and mercy that will endure in us forever.

<<<<<<<<<<<<<<<<<<<<<<<<<<<<<<<<<<<<<<<<<<<

Accept What God Allows

One day this lady was working in a hospital and a position came up that she was interested in, and she applied for it. She was called for an interview, and she asked me to pray. Before I could pray, the Holy Spirit placed in my heart for her to have more faith about the car that he had given her because at that time when the Holy Spirit gave her the desire in her heart for the car, she did not walk out on faith. The Holy Spirit wanted her to have more faith about trying to get this job than what she had when trying to purchase her car. At the same time when the Holy Spirit placed this in my heart, he did not say that she would get the job; it's just that I wanted her to get the job. And by what the Holy Spirit placed in my heart, I just assumed that she would get it. Also, I wanted to see her with that position because I felt like she deserved it, and I wanted so see her with it. She did go to the interview, but she did not receive it. But we know that if God wanted her to have that position, no man would have the power to take it away from God, or even you if he had already blessed you with that position. So when we ask God to lead us and guide us, we have to accept what he allows when there is something that we want and accept that it's not what God wants for us at that time; we should have the faith and know that God has the best interest in our future. He really wanted the young lady to see if she would still have faith and still love him if she did not receive the position. Faith is not rather you get it or not just that you have confidence in God's word. When I spoke with her after, she still said that she still trusts and has faith in God and that she will still allow God to lead her and guide her in the way that he wants her to go. *I thank you, Lord, for the patience. Thank you for allowing me to know how to stand and wait on you, Lord. Thank you for showing me that my faith needed to grow.* She may have been disappointed at that time, but she truly knows who's God. If God is not ready to give me something, then I can stand and wait because I know he must have something better for me if I just stand in faith.

<<<<<<<<<<<<<<<<<<<<<<<<<<<<<<<<<<<<<<<<<<<<<<

Bully

One Sunday, my goddaughter and I were coming from church. We stopped at the store, and when we got home, she had some packages in her hands that she was bringing out of the car. Her hands were full, and she also had her phone in her hand. When she got up on the steps, her phone dropped, and I really wasn't paying that much attention when the phone dropped because I really wasn't interested in her phone dropping. I kept walking up the steps, and I know the Holy Spirit had me to look down where the phone dropped. When I looked down, I did not see the phone but I saw a razor blade. By seeing the blade, I knew that it had to have fallen out of the phone. So I asked her what she was doing with it. At first she did not respond, so I asked her again. She said this young lady at school was bothering her, and that she was afraid of her. I asked her why she did not mention it to me, even though she already did. She said she felt as if I was not going to do anything about it and that she did not want her mother involved. Though at one time she did mention that a young lady was bothering her, but I did not take it seriously because in school, you would not think that you would have to take things so serious. When she told me that if the young lady did approach her, she would be afraid of her. And the young lady said in the school bus that she was going to cut her and said some other things to her and to other people about what she was going to do to her. So she said that's why she had the blade in her phone because she knew the young lady was going to hurt her because of her size, if it came to that. She would respond back with the razor blade also. I asked her if she knew what she was going to get herself into if anything happed. They would not look at the fact that she was being bullied for a period of time, they would just see two people fighting, and they would not want to know what happened or even try to find out why it occurred. That's why I am glad that I serve a superGod. I know if it wasn't for my God keeping a close watch for my daughter, there may have been things that could have happened that they both would have been sorry for. I thanked God for the young lady and my goddaughter, and I'm glad that God was in the midst of it all. That's why he said grace and mercy would follow you all the days of your life. Now tell me that grace and mercy was not following them.

God, I thank you for leading me and teaching me how to pray. I thank you for leading me and teaching me how to plead the blood over my family. I thank you, God, for teaching me how to seek after your heart, and, God, not only seeking after your heart I give my heart to you. God, I see why I love you the way I do because you take care of my family in situations that I am not aware of, or that I wouldn't even imagine could be going on. God, I know that I am not perfect, but thank you for using me in spite of. God, you placed in my heart that you want parents to raise a child in a way so when they get out they will know how to live. God, if I did not train my children the way that I should have, forgive me, Lord, because now I know to train them in the likeness of you, and they will know how to handle themselves out in the cold world.

Yes, God knows that we are loving parents, God knows that we are good parents, but God knows that we are not training our children in the way that they should go. That's God's way because we want to bring up our children the way we want to but not the way God wants us to. "Train up a child in the way he should go: and when he is old, he will not depart from it" (Prov. 22:6).